INSIDE THE ROPES

INSIDE THE ROPES

Arthur Mercante

with Phil Guarnieri

foreword by **Bert Randolph Sugar**

McBooks Press, Inc | Ithaca, NY

Published by McBooks Press 2006
Copyright © 2006 Arthur Mercante and Phil Guarnieri

Cover Photo: AP/WIDE WORLD PHOTOS
Dust jacket and text design: Panda Musgrove

ISBN: 978-1-59013-126-8
1-59013-126-6

Library of Congress Cataloging-in-Publication Data

Mercante, Arthur, 1920-
  Inside the ropes / by Arthur Mercante with Phil Guarnieri.
    p. cm.
  ISBN-13: 978-1-59013-126-8 (hardcover : alk. paper)
  ISBN-10: 1-59013-126-6
  1. Mercante, Arthur, 1920- 2.   Boxing referees—United States—Biography.
I. Guarnieri, Phil, 1957- II. Title.
  GV1132.M45M47 2006
  796.83092—dc22

                              2005033981

Distributed to the trade by National Book Network, Inc.
15200 NBN Way, Blue Ridge Summit, PA 17214
800-462-6420

Additional copies of this book may be ordered from any bookstore or directly from McBooks Press, Inc., ID Booth Building, 520 North Meadow St., Ithaca, NY 14850. Please include $5.00 postage and handling with mail orders. New York State residents must add sales tax to total remittance (books & shipping). All McBooks Press publications can also be ordered by calling toll-free 1-888-BOOKS11 (1-888-266-5711). Please call to request a free catalog.

Visit the McBooks Press website at www.mcbooks.com.

Printed in the United States of America

9 8 7 6 5 4 3 2 1

CONTENTS

foreword

Back in the long-long ago, about the time Adam first heard the siren call of the apple salesman, 1938 to be exact, boxing manager "Dumb" Dan Morgan was asked his opinion of referees. New York's referees, to be specific. "Dumb" Dan, who came by his nickname dishonestly, never failing to get up to speak at the sight of half a grapefruit, could hardly contain himself, nor his metaphors, answering: "They're as scarce as fleas on eels. That's how scarce outstanding referees are in New York . . . They're all good, but not one of them stands out. That is, stands out like a pumpkin in a crate of tangerines."

But "Dumb" Dan's comment was before Arthur Mercante Sr. Before he had reffed hundreds of fights and so many title bouts the bookkeeper's mind rattled at the number—somewhere between 110 and 145, depending upon who was keeping score. And before he had become the most famous third man since Harry Lime.

Those fortunate to have seen Arthur Mercante Sr. in action had the pleasure of witnessing a professional who exerted absolute authority and decisiveness in his actions. Breaching no quarrel with his refereeing, Mercante would rarely have to use more than one word to enforce boxing's rules and regulations or one eye to break up clinches where the combatants had seemed as inseparable as two wire coat hangers. In short, Arthur Mercante Sr. could take his place in the ring and make any dues-paying fan feel good.

And while he served as the middleman in the unfolding dramas of a long laundry list of great fights—such as Ali–Frazier I, Patterson–Johansson II, Foreman–Frazier I, Ali–Norton III and Arguello–Escalera, amongst many—Mercante, unlike so many other referees, was never involved in controversy of any kind. Granted, controversy is to boxing what garnish is to a martini, enlivening it, Mercante never drank from its cup, his professionalism enabling him to escape the fate of many of his brethren, controversies which left them feeling like flies in soup, attracting attention and comment but hardly enjoying it.

Over the years reverence due Mercante's accomplishments has increased. And when a group photo is taken of all the great "touch-gloves-and-come-out-fighting" brigade, Arthur Mercante will not only be in the picture, he will be front and center. For such are his entitlements that the U.S. Post Office has issued commemorative stamps for achievements far less noteworthy.

Boxing fans who delight in boxing delicacies will delight in Mercante's book, one which, when opened, fills our nostrils with the odor of boxing past, much like an old antique trunk which, when opened, overwhelms us with its memories. For this book is better than a ringside seat; it takes us into the ring itself. Mercante's ring.

Bert Randolph Sugar

Chappaqua, New York

preface

For many years now my family, friends and colleagues have urged me to tell my life story as a boxing referee. For one reason or another I've always put the telling off.

French Field Marshall Henri Philippe Pétain may not have had the most admirable politics (he was a member of the Vichy government in WWII) but he knew the value of honesty after the fact. When asked why he never wrote his memoirs he replied, "Because I have nothing to hide." This always seemed like sound reasoning to me. But in September 2001 I retired as the man "inside the ropes," having officiated for seven decades in the amateur and professional ranks and I realized it was time to put it all down on paper. And so I have: my childhood in Brockton, Massachusetts, and later Brooklyn, New York; my military service in WWII; my debut as professional boxing referee; the championship fights I officiated or attended that riveted the world and are now an indelible part of sports' history; and the larger than life personalities I've known in boxing, a few who are as known and renowned as kings, presidents or popes.

I was privileged to be part of boxing during its most glorious and storied years. I hope what emerges in the pages that follow is an entertaining chronicle of my life and career, its blemishes as well as its accomplishments, told in a style that bristles with the flying fists and unsparing drama of the prize ring itself.

These days boxing no longer inhabits the lofty pedestal in the sports world it once did, but I'm always fascinated by the extent our culture still embraces the drama of the prize ring. In a society that reflexively denounces violence, there is still something primitively captivating about two combatants stripped down, fists encased in leather, ready to do battle. Just look at Hollywood. The movie moguls still churn out more movies about boxing than about all other sports combined.

Acknowledgements are a necessary part of every book and this one has its share. I want to thank my agent, Jake Elwell, for his consideration, patience and professionalism in guiding me in this new, strange world of publishing. I'm also grateful to Theresa A. Sciarrotta who helped type the early manuscript and to Karen A. Graham who was involved in the later stages of transcribing written notes to a computer disc.

Most importantly I recognize my family. To four terrific young men I'm proud to call my sons—Glenn, James, Arthur and Tom—for their support and encouragement. And to my grandchildren, Brittany and Dylan, who inspired "Papa Referee" to share with them these stories of his life. Finally, the light of my life, my companion through life's joys and griefs, my wife, Gloria, to whom I dedicate this book, with all my love and gratitude.

INSIDE THE ROPES

PROLOGUE

T HE WHOLE WORLD was watching. You could just feel it. There was evidence of it wherever you looked in Madison Square Garden on the night of March 8, 1971: the low buzzing hum of thousands of fans crammed into the arena; the small army of reporters, all fitted in red and yellow jackets, garrisoning themselves around the perimeter of the ring; the incessant blinding flashes of countless cameras recording the event for posterity.

Checking the resistance of the ring ropes, I could see the tall, angular form of John Condon, director of public relations for Madison Square Garden boxing, bustling in and out of the press rows, impatiently barking out orders and searching intently for unwanted intruders. Directly below me, Don Dunphy—"The Voice of Boxing"—was doing last-minute preparations with actor Burt Lancaster for their color commentary on the big fight. Looking beyond them and scanning over the sea of humanity that engulfed the Garden, I noted the galaxy of Hollywood celebrities, politicians and sports personalities.

In their midst stood the lonely 20 x 20–foot boxing ring that seemed to draw everything to it. Even Frank Sinatra was snared by its pull. Commissioned by *Life* magazine to photograph the fight, the famous singer and actor kept revolving around the platform, snapping pictures—a lone human satellite on a special mission, captured along with the rest of the world by the bout's massive gravitational field.

The event had reached international proportions, and preparations to bring its violent images to the whole world had been carefully and painstakingly mapped out. The telecommunication signal from the Garden was to be picked up by the AT&T building on Canal Street where it was to be transmitted instantly on long telephone lines throughout the United States and thirty-five other countries, reaching an unprecedented audience of at least three hundred million viewers.

Amid the deafening noise I nodded to the dapper veteran ring announcer, Johnny Addie, who walked to the microphone and called the honor roll of the ring greats of yesteryear. They were all there: Jack Dempsey, Gene Tunney, Joe Louis, Sugar Ray Robinson, Willie Pep, Archie Moore, Rocky Graziano and more. As the parade of champions made its way across the ring, I began to feel warm, nervous droplets of sweat form on my forehead. My palms were moist with perspiration, my throat dry as a desert wind. I pressed my tongue to the roof of my mouth to get a squirt of saliva and then swallowed hard.

This would be the biggest night in my professional life, and while being a boxing referee was second nature to me, I realized, being only human, that I could not remain totally unaffected by the great drama unfolding before my eyes. Within minutes, I would be right in the center of it, an integral character in the most riveting event in ring history.

My day had begun ordinarily enough. Arriving at work at 8 AM sharp at 485 Madison Avenue in New York City, where I worked in institutional sales for the Schaefer Brewing Company, I poured myself a cup of steaming hot coffee, mixing it with a little cream and a dab of brown sugar. Opening my copy of the *Daily News*, I quickly turned to the sports section and saw it was filled with coverage for the big fight: Muhammad Ali versus Joe Frazier for the undisputed Heavyweight Championship of the World. It would be the first time two undefeated champions would be fighting for the most prized title in all of sports. This was a fight that needed no publicity, but it got reams of it day in and day out.

Amidst all the analysis and predictions was an article on the most likely referee for the big bout. The piece focused on seven captioned photographs of the leading candidates for the job. I quickly spotted my picture and then read everything I could about the fight with a growing, but still suppressed, excitement.

Of course I was dying to get the assignment. Everyone was. But as badly as I wanted to officiate the bout, I saw no sense in getting worked up worrying about it. After all, I consoled myself, it was an honor just to be considered for something of this magnitude. The minutes, then the hours, ticked away interminably. It was a hell of a way to spend the next eight hours.

At four o'clock the phone rang, ending the suspense I pretended not to feel. It was Commissioner Edwin Dooley of the New York State Athletic Commission. He was short and to the point: "Mr. Mercante, it's yours. Report for assignment at the Garden at 6 PM."

"Yes sir," I replied with what I thought, under the circumstances, was commendable brevity. "It's yours," meant I was the one. I had landed right in the middle of the fight of the century. I could hardly believe it. When I hurried out of the office that late afternoon I felt like I was floating on air.

I walked briskly to Fifty-ninth Street and Seventh Avenue, to the New York Athletic Club. As was my habit before a big fight, I took a hot steam bath to relax. After a few stretching exercises it was down to the dining room where I wolfed down a minute steak, chasing it with a tall glass of ice water. Then I hurried to the downtown subway, praying I wouldn't bump into anyone I knew, and sped off to my date with destiny.

Things were happening so quickly my brain was flooded with a thousand thoughts. I desperately tried to sort through them only to be jolted by the shout of the conductor announcing Penn Station. Bolting from the train I raced up the platform steps two at a time and made my way into the Garden through the entrance on Thirty-third Street.

I was ushered through a thick network of security personnel and into a dressing room, where Deputy Commissioner Frank Morris went through the mandatory recitation of the New York State Athletic Commission rules. I listened dutifully, although I had heard it recited a thousand times before and could've mouthed the worlds right along with Frank.

During the preliminary bouts I began to change into my referee uniform, double knotting my shoelaces and carefully adjusting my black bow tie. As usual, I followed my pre-fight exercise regimen: a few stretches and pushups to warm up my muscles, then some brisk walking in the back hallways, and I was ready. All that remained was to wait for the main event.

Finally it was time. As I climbed through the ropes that evening to referee the richest, most lucrative sporting event in history, everything seemed so surreal. It was not only a night of high finance but high fashion. Beautiful, statuesque women were dressed in ornate but scanty designer gowns. Toots Shor, the legendary sports restaurateur, had brought in three busloads of customers dressed in black ties. The whole scene looked like something you would expect to see at Academy Awards night rather than fight night at the Garden.

The lights dimmed. For a few moments I stood alone in the squared circle; then, suddenly, there was an explosive roar from the crowd. Making his way toward the ring, surrounded by a huge entourage, was Muhammad Ali. In keeping with the eye-popping décor of the evening, he was resplendent in a lavish red robe, matching red velvet trunks and white tasseled shoes. Joe Frazier soon followed and, not to be upstaged, was outfitted in a bright green robe and gold brocade trunks. Ali looked relaxed and playful; Frazier, grim and determined. Both fighters appeared to be in magnificent physical condition.

As I called the fighters to the center of the ring, more than twenty thousand people in the Garden crouched on the edges of their seats, watching in tense, mounting and irrepressible excitement. It was the same for hundreds of millions of others around the globe, watching on closed-circuit television. As I stood between the fighters to give the pre-fight instructions, my nervousness had vanished, supplanted by a feeling of confident command. I knew I was ready.

Given time to reflect on the matter, I would have no doubt thought, as I did later, what a long road it had been to this incredible night. It was a journey that began a half century earlier in Brockton, Massachusetts, a city twenty-five miles from Boston, just south of Cape Cod, a city of industry, a sports-crazed city where, by temperament and breeding, boxing got into my blood. And it was a city where, amid the noise and sweat of this hardworking blue-collar community, I heard my first calling to the ring . . .

chapter 1

BEGINNINGS

My father, Ralph Mercante, was a laborer in the shoe factories of Brockton, Massachusetts. He sweated hard and long hours to put bread on the table and a roof over our heads. I remember watching him hunched over the bed laster machine, nails protruding from his lips as he molded leather into finely made shoes. My father took great pride in his work. Throughout his life he never thought of himself as a shoemaker but, rather, as a craftsman of leather.

During my youth there was little money to spare in the Mercante household. We saved whatever we could. Instead of buying things, my father would make them. One day he made me a football. I was beaming ear-to-ear when I showed it to my friend. But when I tossed it to him it bounced off his chest and rolled under a passing trolley car. With one loud burst, my football was a mere memory.

I was devastated and could not bring myself to ask my father to make another. But seeing my forlorn face, my father knew something was wrong.

"What's the matter Arturo?" he asked. "Tell your father."

Reluctantly, I told him about the football.

"Don't be upset, son," he said consolingly. "I'll make you a new one." With the shape and pattern now memorized by his fingertips, he fashioned a football superior to even the original. My father's hands, they were gifted.

Without an education, a man had to live by the strength of his back or the dexterity of his fingers. It was a lesson my father learned very early in life. Born in Campobasso, Italy, a little town just southeast of Rome, my father grew up in a religious, hardworking family. They were very poor so when my father was just fourteen years of age, he set off for America to make his way in the world. He arrived on Ellis Island in the late autumn of 1904, just one year before my mother and her family would also arrive in the United States.

This was a time of great migration to the New World. Immigrants from southern and eastern Europe flooded the shores of the "Land of the Free." They came to find a better life for their families and themselves. They spoke a foreign tongue and were virtually penniless. But they were rich in dreams and wealthy in their willingness to work as hard as they could to make them a reality.

Many years later, in 1997, I was awarded the Ellis Island Medal of Honor, which recognizes the contributions of the individual to America but also acknowledges the influence of one's ancestors toward making this country the great nation it is. As I overlooked the great New York Harbor where my parents first arrived almost a century earlier, I was nearly overcome with emotion. Without their courage and sacrifices, my life here would not have been possible. The medal was awarded to me, but in my heart I consecrated it to the memory of my mother and father.

My father's early years in America are not entirely traceable, for even in the narrow circle of family, living testimony becomes lost and memories are forgotten over time. We do know he first lived on Amsterdam Avenue in New York City and that he apprenticed himself to various shoemakers and learned his trade. In time, he saved enough to open his own shop. Always on the lookout for better opportunities, he learned of a textile city known as Brockton, Massachusetts, a melting pot where Irish, Italians, Jews and a smattering of Scandinavians settled to find gainful employment, mostly in the thriving shoemaking industry there.

My mother's family, the Montaganos, on the other hand, moved to Brockton in 1905, a year after my father arrived on Ellis Island. My mother, Angelina, was the daughter of a migrant farmer from Italy who had settled in Brazil. At the turn of the century, Brockton was made up of large tracts of farmland. Feeling the allure of America, my maternal grandfather picked up his family and left Brazil for the United States, never to look back.

My mother spent her formative years in Brockton. She was a kindly, intelligent woman whose diction in both Italian and English was nearly flawless. By chance, both Mom and Pop ended up working for the Walkover Shoe Company, where my father arranged an introduction and, according to custom, obtained her father's permission to court his daughter. On December 4, 1917, their marriage was solemnized at the local Roman Catholic Church.

The newlyweds continued working at the shoe company, pooling their money and saving what they could for the future. They became very friendly with another young Italian couple, Pierino and Pasqualena Marchegiano, whose firstborn son would become one of boxing history's most celebrated champions under the name Rocky Marciano.

In the years that followed, my mother gave birth to three healthy boys: Ralph, born in 1918; me in 1920; and the youngest, Alfred, in 1926. My mother was thrifty and cooked nourishing meals for us. She was particularly fastidious in making sure all her boys were neat and well dressed, a habit of good grooming that would remain with me all my life. Both my parents gave us a lot of love and instilled in us good moral values and an appreciation of the importance of hard, honest work. What more does any child need, really? Today, I am often asked who my boyhood heroes were. Because the first decade of my life was known as the "Golden Age of Sports" people naturally assume that I will cite Babe Ruth, Jack Dempsey, Red Grange or Johnny Weissmuller, all great idols of that gilded age. I looked up to them all, but my heroes not only lived under the same roof as me, they provided it. No stars in my firmament shined brighter than my mother and father.

During my earliest years, I was severely bowlegged. I got around all right, but my legs bowed outward to such a degree I looked disabled. My mother took me to several doctors, but they all seemed stumped. My mother started feeding me some homemade nutritional brew. The remedy worked, and by the age of six or seven my legs almost miraculously straightened out. Although it was never formerly diagnosed, I figure I must have had rickets. Whatever the cause of the deformity, I'm glad it cleared up before I entered the Golden Gloves or I would have been tagged, God forbid, as "The Bowlegged Bomber."

Brockton was a great sports city that produced a number of high school championship teams, especially in football. It was no mystery then, why I grew up loving to play sports. I was never big, but I was strong and had the quick reflexes and instincts of an athlete. As a youngster I was even able to parlay this athleticism into tap dancing. By the age of ten I could really tap. When my father opened his shoe repair shop, I would not only shine customers' shoes but entertain them as well. While spit shining their shoes, I would go into a whole tap routine, rhythmically snapping the shoe shine cloth as I danced. The men loved it and gave me a five-cent tip. For another nickel, I would grasp the metal sides on the two-step shoe shining stand, tip up into a handstand and remain upright for a full minute.

But it wasn't football, baseball, acrobatics or tap dancing that most engrossed my youthful attentions. My true love was boxing. My uncle, Joe Monte, was a professional in the light heavyweight and, later, heavyweight ranks who was good enough to have fought two champions, Max Schmeling and James J. Braddock, three times! Nearly as formidable was my Uncle Neib Montagano, an ex-marine who had been interested in boxing for years. In me they found an apt and willing pupil. My uncles had me throwing jabs and hooks almost before I could walk. This early exposure to boxing had a tremendous influence on me. I grew up across the road from a farm where boxers like my Uncle Neib trained. The ring was situated in the middle of a pine grove. Most of the boxers training there were heavyweights, and with their sun-tanned physiques and their bulging, well-defined muscles, they seemed to me to be the ultimate gladiators. I was enthralled by their skill, their guts. I could hardly wait to grow up and be just like them.

As a special treat, my uncles would often take me along in Uncle Joe's Model T to the gym in Boston where Uncle Joe trained. There, I would keenly observe the fighters working out. I would hear the rat-a-tat-tat of the light striking-bags, the heavy sandbag's chain clanging with every punch to its midsection and the metronomic beat of leather jump ropes hitting the wooden floor. It was all music to my ears, wonderful enchanting music.

The fighters who trained in that Boston gym were top-shelf performers; a few even became world champions. There was Jack Sharkey, who had fought the great Jack Dempsey and would one day be heavyweight champion himself, and Lou Broulliard, who would win the world's welterweight title. I also vividly recall seeing the unfortunate Ernie Schaaf, a strapping heavyweight contender who would tragically lose his life in a bout with the Italian Goliath, Primo Carnera.

Thanks to these experiences, I really developed the itch to fight—a little too much, in fact. One day when I was about eight years old, my uncles took me to a playground for some exercise and recreation. Among the children playing there was a tough-looking Irish kid who was bullying the other kids around. His belligerence began to get under Uncle Neib's skin, which, admittedly, was a tad thin. Grabbing me by the arm, Neib whispered into my ear, "Arthur, see that kid over there? Why don't you go spar with him." I didn't need to be prodded and neither did the Irish kid when I invited him to square off.

He started flailing away at me with wild punches, all of which I easily blocked or avoided. With my uncles looking on approvingly, I began to counter him with telling punches of my own. Uncles Neib and Joe, obviously delighted that their lessons had paid off so handsomely, cheered me on like a couple of school kids.

The mismatch ended when the boy began bawling loudly and, out of nowhere, his mother appeared, screaming bloody murder and threatening to have my uncles arrested for encouraging children to fight. Neib and Joe scooped me up, and we were off like cat burglars in the night. At a safe distance they put me down and congratulated me on such a good showing. I felt like I was ten feet tall. There was no greater badge of honor than the praise of my uncles.

Unfortunately, by the time I was nine or ten years old, my street fighting became something of a habit, especially after my father relocated the family to Brooklyn. My strong Massachusetts accent got me into a lot of trouble with the boys there. It didn't help that my mother insisted on dressing me in a Buster Brown collar and tie. The local toughs pegged me for a sissy, and I had to fight almost daily to prove them wrong. Soon the word was out: Watch out for that kid who talks funny and dresses funnier—he packs a real wallop.

Mom and Pop were very disturbed about my constant fighting. Pop tried to channel my aggressive instincts into organized activity. One Saturday morning he took me to the Bedford Branch YMCA and asked if there was a boy's program.

Sorry, the man said, it is only set up for men.

The man's name was Howard Anderson, the general manager and a true gentleman. When my father suggested there was a need for a boy's program, Mr. Anderson agreed. As a result, they started a Saturday morning boys' division of which I was the first charter member. The program was soon successful, and within a year they decided to build an annex to the main building. It became known as the Bedford YMCA Boys Branch. Frequenting it was a great experience for me and solidified my growing interest in health and physical education.

Despite his best efforts, my father was not wholly successful in diverting my attention from fighting, not by a long shot. In the 1930s, the nation was mired in the worst depression of its history, and that hungry time proved fertile ground for boxing. Fight clubs sprouted like mushrooms after a heavy summer rain. Boxing was never bigger than it was then, and I longed to be part of the action.

It was always a treat when Uncle Joe took me to the annual Boxing Writers' Dinner in New York City. Seeing so many great fighters gathered in one room—Mickey Walker, Barney Ross, Henry Armstrong, Tony Canzoneri, Jimmy McLarnin and many more—sent chills up and down my spine. The biggest thrill of all, though, was when the newly crowned Heavyweight Champion of the World walked into the room. If you were a sports-minded teenager living in New York back in 1935, you wanted to grow up to be either Lou Gehrig, the great Yankee ballplayer, or Max Baer. I chose Baer.

When you first met Max Baer, he just overwhelmed you with his rugged good looks and overpowering physical appearance. With huge sloping shoulders tapering down to a thirty-one-inch waist, Baer, at six feet three inches and 220 sculpted pounds, looked as if he was picked out of central casting to play the role of Heavyweight Champion. But it was his larger-than-life personality even more than his physique that made him a beloved and colorful character. A laugh a minute, scandalously irreverent, always engaging, Baer remains one of the most magnetic personalities I have ever encountered in sports. Max Baer truly believed it when he said, "What's the use of being alive if you can't have fun?"

Everyone seemed to agree that Baer would be champion as long as he wanted to. In the ring, his chin seemed impervious to leather, and his roundhouse right hand is still regarded by fight historians as one of the hardest punches ever thrown. But a funny thing happened to Baer on his way to boxing immortality. A tall, rugged, unheralded heavyweight named James J. Braddock came off the docks and the welfare rolls to beat the 10–1 odds against him and outpoint the champion in

Baer's very first title defense. Boxing would not see a bigger upset until James "Buster" Douglas knocked out Mike Tyson fifty-five years later.

Later that same year, Joe Louis, barely twenty-one years old, would destroy Baer in less than four rounds of fighting. Max waved to the crowd as the referee counted him out and said afterwards that anyone who wanted to see the execution of Max Baer would have to pay more than the cost of a ringside seat. After that, he was never again a serious contender. The Clown Prince of Boxing was only fifty when he died of a heart attack. Baer's life, like his boxing career, shone brightly, but all too briefly.

Attending boxing events made me more determined than ever to make a name for myself in the ring. You needed to be eighteen years of age to be able to enter the Gloves. But I was too anxious to wait another two years. At sixteen, two years seemed an eternity. So unbeknownst to my folks, I took my older brother Ralph's ID and got my passport into amateur boxing.

In 1936, I entered the New York Golden Gloves Tournament under the name "Ralph Mercante." The competition was ferocious, but I was trained to a razor's edge. As I look back to those long ago days, I'm astonished how fearlessly I fought and how mean and rough I could be. I just didn't like anyone in the ring with me. I had, as they say today, bad intentions. I also brought along my cheering section: guys from the neighborhood who would come to the fights to root me on. Shouts of "Get him, Art—kill him, Art" filled the arena, which had the officials scratching their heads, since I had been introduced as Ralph.

I scored four straight knockouts before I was outpointed in the quarterfinals by twenty-four-year-old Jerry Fiorello, who not only won the championship but also would make a name for himself in the pros as a real tough club fighter.

Managers were always on the lookout for good prospects, and several of them lobbied me to turn pro. I was flattered; my father was horrified. "Absolutely not, Arturo! Those men, they don't care what happens to you!" he said. "They just want to make money watching you get your brains beat in."

I argued with him, pointing out I had done very well in the Gloves and had come out unharmed.

"Arturo," he said with patience and wisdom I did not fully appreciate until years later, "there is a big difference between the amateurs and the real pros. One day this country is going to come out of this depression, and your future is going to depend on you using your head, not your fists, and that means learning in school and not fighting in the ring."

I must admit, at the time, I wasn't happy about my father's decision, but being an obedient son, I bowed to his wishes.

With my boxing career over before it had even begun, I was off to New York University. Although I was done with boxing competitively, I kept close to the sport and based my physical conditioning on a boxing regimen. I believed then, and still do today, that there is no better way to get in top physical condition than by doing a boxing workout daily and religiously. Because of this conviction, health and physical conditioning became a way of life for me.

chapter 2

FIGHTING FOR UNCLE SAM

L IFE WENT ON pretty much as normal. I went to classes at New York University, won first place in a diving championship with the university swim team and enjoyed a wholesome home life with my folks and my two brothers. Like many Italian families, we were very close. But this rather uneventful, non-assuming existence was to take a dramatic turn for us and millions of other American families.

It was a Sunday afternoon in December 1941, and, as was our custom, our family gathered around the table for a bowl of my mother's homemade spaghetti. The radio broadcast in the background was interrupted with the news bulletin that the Japanese had launched a devastating surprise attack on our naval forces at Pearl Harbor. Like most Americans, we had never even heard of Pearl Harbor, but we all knew what the news meant. The next morning President Roosevelt delivered his immortal "Day of Infamy" speech. America was at war.

Being young, I felt very excited about the talk of war. I did not appreciate until I had boys of my own how hard the news must have been for Mom and Pop with two sons of draft age and another just two or three years away. It must be a terribly hard thing to see one's children go off to war knowing they may never come back.

But I couldn't wait for Uncle Sam to call me, and in April 1942 I joined the United States Navy. When my recruiters learned about my interest in boxing and physical conditioning, they assigned me to the Gene Tunney Physical Fitness Program.

U.S. Navy Captain James Joseph Gene Tunney, former Heavyweight Champion of the World, recruited many of the outstanding athletes of that period to perform the duties of training new servicemen. Eventually, these recruits would be assigned to physically rehabilitate navy veterans who had been wounded and physically impaired in the line of duty.

Training recruits and getting them in shape was the perfect assignment for me. I would stand on a six-foot platform overlooking a sea of three thousand sailors dressed in white tee shirts and white trousers. It must've been quite a sight as I barked out commands through a microphone: "Left jab . . . right cross . . . left hook . . ." making them really work up a sweat. It was quite a heady experience for me to have so many men under my command. I was, after all, only twenty-two years old.

I also got the wonderful opportunity to meet Gene Tunney himself. I really admired Tunney. He had been a marvelously skilled boxer who was always in top condition and managed to leave boxing with both his money and marbles intact—in this business, no mean accomplishment.

Seeing Tunney up close and shaking his large hand was a huge thrill. He was an impressive, imposing looking man. Big and tall, with a handsome face that was amazingly unmarked for a guy who had fought Harry Greb five times and Jack Dempsey twice. It was also a nostalgic moment for me. Among my earliest memories was listening to our old radio gramophone as Tunney fought the famous "Battle of the Long Count" with Jack Dempsey and also the last bout of his career against durable Tom Heeney, aptly called the "Hard Rock from Down Under," who was ground into powder by the champion's bristling, two-fisted combinations. Sam Taub, the great radio sports announcer, broadcast those fights, and I still remember my excitement with every punch he described.

But all wasn't so rosy in the navy. Under Gene Tunney's program, I was later stationed at the Naval Training Station in Farragut, Idaho, named after Admiral David Farragut who was immortalized for saying, "Damn the torpedoes, full speed ahead," at the sea battle of Mobile Bay during the Civil War. It was quite an impressive operation, Farragut being the second largest naval base in the United States. I was sent there as part of the navy's supervisory staff, overseeing the athletic program for their recruits. All the coaches there went under the title "Chief Specialist" and my specialty was, of course, the manly art of self-defense. Just as before, I coached boxing. I made fast friends there; some friendships lasted a lifetime. We were all mostly young guys, and being far from home, companionship and a feeling of community was important. I got along famously with everyone—except one guy, a big Texan named Cheatum.

The Texan was the base's football coach who I dubbed "Wolf Larson," a character right out of the pages of Jack London's novel *The Sea Wolf.* A surly, nasty, first-class misanthrope, who took pleasure in nursing hatreds, he was undoubtedly the most unpleasant human being I ever knew. And coming from the cutthroat world of boxing, that's no mean statement. I don't know exactly when it all started between us, but it became obvious that Cheatum couldn't stand the living sight of me. He never said anything to my face, but when he condescended to mention me to others, I was told he referred to me as "that dirty dago."

I kept my cool. I had matured quite a bit. Instead of responding with my fists, I now walked away from trouble and tried to live my life in a way that was respectful to others and avoided confrontation. Maybe it was the navy, or maybe the Golden Gloves had knocked all the aggression out of me, or maybe the gentlemanly manner of Gene Tunney had more influence on me than I realized. Whatever it was, it had been years since I hit anyone outside the ring, and I was proud of my new self-control. But the burly Texan began to test my patience when I heard he was bad-mouthing me all over the base.

I asked one of my buddies, who knew Cheatum, what the Texan had against me.

"Well, Art," he laconically replied, "you're breathing: that's strike number one. Second," he said, grinning, "you're a coach in a different sport: strike number two. Third, you're Italian: strike number three—you're out." Apparently, being of Italian descent was an unpardonable sin in the Cheatum catechism.

"Yeah," I said angrily, "well I'm not apologizing for being Italian, and I'm certainly not going to stop breathing to make him feel better about me."

"Oh, just ignore him, Art. Everyone knows he's a son of a bitch. In fact, if you are going to be bad-mouthed, I can't think of anyone better to be bad-mouthed by than him," he said, laughing.

"O.K., I'll ignore him. But if he starts calling me names or using ethnic slurs to my face, that Texan will wish he was back at the Alamo with Davy Crockett."

As luck would have it, I found myself sitting opposite Cheatum at the dining table. I could see something wasn't agreeing with him—and it wasn't the chow. All through the meal he kept muttering under his breath about dagos and dirty guineas. Since I was the only Italian at the table, his object of derision was no mystery. My dining companions shifted uncomfortably in their seats and eyeballed each other nervously. I did nothing. But as I walked back to my quarters, I did a slow burn. My face felt beet red, and I was starting to brim over with rage—who the hell did Cheatum think he was?

I decided to pay a personal call to Cheatum—Mr. Wolf Larson himself—whose quarters were right down the hall from my own, and perhaps, over a cup of tea, have a heart-to-heart talk. When he opened the door, Cheatum wasted no time in making me feel welcomed. "What the fuck do you want Mercante?" he said loudly.

I pushed my way in and said, "Look, you are going to apologize to me right here and now for all the dirty things you've been saying behind my back." The Lone Star prick began showering me with the worst invective imaginable, salting his language with his usual ethnic slurs. I returned his salutations with a robust display of vulgarities to show I had learned more than just drilling in the navy.

The next thing I knew, he grabbed a metal chair and with a rage bordering on the homicidal swung it at my head. I managed to grab the chair with my right hand and throw a left hook that landed with all I owned on his right eye socket, which exploded in a waterfall of blood. As he was going down, he grabbed me by my shirt, now drenched with his blood, and we went crashing over his furniture and down on the floor with me on top. I felt like I was in one of those saloon brawls in an old cowboy movie.

We made quite a row—coaches rushed in to pry us apart. Cheatum's eye was a gory mess and my shirt was drenched with his blood. Several buddies dragged me back to my quarters to cool me off. To avoid a summary court-martial for both of us, a story was concocted that the eye injury was a result of a softball game where my bat slipped, hitting the catcher, Cheatum, in the eye—an unfortunate accident.

The medics who did the stitching looked very skeptical, but the cause of the injury was recorded as an accident in a ball game. Cheatum never gave me any more trouble after that; not that we began exchanging Christmas cards, but there was a cold cease-fire. A short time after our violent interlude, Cheatum was brought up on charges of abuse and cruelty to the recruits and given a dishonorable discharge from the navy.

In my little group I became the camp hero, the guy who squashed the class bully. But I wasn't proud of what happened and tried to downplay it. It would be the only time, as an adult, I ever hit someone outside the ring. From then on my association with fighting would be strictly inside the ropes.

It was in the service that I got my first taste of refereeing boxing matches. I refereed hundreds of bouts, which served as a great training ground and learning experience for my professional career later on. I found that not only did I really enjoy refereeing but also that I had a knack, or a natural instinct, for officiating. Refereeing those matches, I never dreamed I would referee professionally, much less referee some of the most storied fights in boxing history.

My experience with boxing in the service was not strictly limited to training recruits, meeting champions and refereeing bouts between servicemen. I actually got an opportunity to put the gloves on again as a boxer, or at least a sparring partner. Serving at our base was one-time Middleweight Champion Fred Apostoli. Apostoli was still fighting professionally and was training for a fight against Ken Overlin, a talented, quick-moving boxer who was briefly champion himself. Getting Fred ready for that fight became a matter of naval pride. He was, after all, one of our own.

Apostoli had been a great, though unheralded, champion in the late 1930s. After fighting two great fights against Billy Conn before Billy moved up in weight to the light heavyweight division, Fred, though a tad past his prime, was still considered one of the best middleweights in the world in 1942. I was one of three sparring partners assigned to get him in top condition for the Overlin fight.

Raised in an orphanage, Apostoli was even tougher than the life he lived. With his hairy chest, well-muscled body and bowlegged walk (Fred always walked as if he had just climbed off a horse), Apostoli would make a marine sergeant think twice before starting a bar fight with him.

Fred would begin the day's sparring with a spirited workout against the base's two-hundred-pound heavyweight champion. Despite being outweighed by nearly forty pounds, Apostoli more than held his own. I came next, a middleweight with a combination of speed and power.

What did it feel like to be in the ring with this former champion? Murder would not be too strong a term to describe it. Remember how vicious I said I was in the Golden Gloves? Next to a real pro like Fred Apostoli, I felt like an altar boy. It was hard for me to believe that somebody relatively my size could be so much stronger than I was.

When I fought in the Gloves no one ever hurt me; now even with the heavy padded training gloves, I felt my bones rattle every time Apostoli landed a blow. Pop was right: the difference between the pros and the amateurs was the difference between Mom's Sunday spaghetti and Chef Boyardee.

I was forced to fight all-out or just get blown right out of the ring. While I certainly wasn't in Apostoli's class—not by a long shot—he respected me and thought I had ability. One time he got careless and let his guard down. Instinctively, I fired a right hand with everything I owned. It landed square on Apostoli's chin. His legs wobbled and I grabbed him by the arms to give him support: "Gee, Fred, I'm sorry," I said. "Are you okay?"

Such niceties bothered him more than getting hit. "Quit apologizing, goddamn it. This isn't a card game!" Fred was a hell of a nice guy, but for him the ring was no place for the softhearted.

Looking back, I loved everything about the navy. For some the service is too challenging, too hard a life. But I thrived on the discipline, the regimentation and the exacting demands they made, both physically and psychologically; and the physical rehabilitation of our brave navy men was the most satisfying and rewarding work I was ever involved with. I left the navy with mixed emotions after having thought seriously about making a career of the service. I felt pride in my contributions to the U.S. Navy; and even greater gratitude for what the navy had given me in return. When I had enlisted in April 1942, I went into the navy still a boy; when I was discharged in January 1946, I left a man.

chapter 3
ON MY WAY

AFTER I LEFT the navy in 1946, I was offered a job as a boxing instructor at West Point, the U.S. Military Academy. I was flattered by the offer and very tempted by the annual stipend of $3,728. That sounds, and is, worse than poverty wages today, but sixty years ago it was a pretty fair starting wage.

I was intrigued by the idea of being associated with West Point, where military and patriotic legends like Douglas MacArthur, Dwight Eisenhower and George Patton had begun their military careers. There was an undeniable martial aura about the place, and even when I visit there today I feel the chill of history in my bones.

While I was mulling over the West Point offer, I received an offer from the U.S. Merchant Marine Academy for employment as a varsity boxing coach and a member of their physical education staff. Not only was the academy much closer to where I lived, the salary was better. Practicality won out over romance, and I accepted the position.

Also around this time, I applied and was accepted as a referee for the National Collegiate Boxing Association. College boxing was as popular then as basketball is today, and often the bouts on campus drew bigger crowds than the hoops. Can you imagine that happening today? Consequently, I received a lot of exposure. Soon, to my surprise, I became recognized as boxing's premier college referee. I refereed bouts all over the country, including the U.S. Naval Academy,

West Point, University of Maryland, Georgetown University, Catholic University of America, City College of New York and others.

I also had the opportunity to train the collegians. My boxers participated in various competitions, including the National Intercollegiate Boxing Championships in Wisconsin. It was a great experience for me, both as a coach and referee. All the college boxers were fine, clean-cut boys, and what they lacked in boxing skills they made up for in fighting spirit.

Because of my success and notoriety as a referee on the college circuit, I was soon encouraged to apply to the New York State Athletic Commission (NYSAC) for a professional referee's license. Being a pro referee would put me even closer to the game I loved, and pro refs like Arthur Donovan and Ruby Goldstein were respected boxing figures in their own right. The more I thought about it, the more sense it made. At that time, Robert Christenberry was the chairman of the NYSAC. With high hopes I filled out my application and waited to hear when I would start.

It would be a very long wait. High hopes weren't, it turned out, what greased the gears of the political bureaucracy controlling the boxing apparatus in the Empire State. To become a pro boxing referee you needed connections. In other words, you had to belong to the local Democratic Party or know a political insider willing to pull strings on your behalf. It was the old story—it's not what you know; it's who you know.

When I heard this via the ever-reliable grapevine, I initially dismissed it as baseless nonsense: What in the world did politics have to do with boxing? When it came to pure naiveté, I admit I was a contender for the championship of the world. I believed the right people were bound to see my qualifications and experience and would come knocking on my door fairly begging me to put all that to work for them. I guess Fred Apostoli hadn't whacked all the Pollyanna out of me. Obviously, I still had a lot to learn about the world.

Whenever I would inquire about the status of my license application, the excuses were always the same: "There are no openings," "We have enough referees right now," or the ever popular "Keep in touch; something is bound to come your way." Soon enough it became obvious that their excuses were downright lies. If there were no openings, why were there new licensed referees every year? It took a while, but I came to see that "keep in touch" really meant that I was "out of touch" and shouldn't bother calling back.

What I found especially galling was that these new referees did not have nearly the qualifications or experience I had. This wasn't just my opinion but also that of people in professional boxing who told me I was getting the shaft. Before I knew it, 1949 became '50, then '51, '52 and '53, and I was no closer to wearing a bow tie for pay than before. I felt as if I was drowning in quicksand without a rope in sight.

Looking back, I now realize that my earlier achievements had left me unprepared to maneuver effectively around these roadblocks. Frankly, success had come a little too easy for me. As a youngster, my athletic talents won the respect of my peers. In the service, I was singled out to train thousands of recruits, many of them older than I, for the rigors of military life. After leaving the navy, I was courted by two prestigious military academies. Not long after starting to referee college matches, I went to the front of the line as the top intercollegiate referee.

All my life I had just performed to the best of my ability and good things happened. Now I was coming to the sinking realization that no matter how hard I worked, how much experience I had, or what my qualifications were, there were other considerations that trumped all that, which could keep me from ever getting a license. As long as I remained outside the inner circle, the system, the privileged elite or whatever you want to call it, I'd never be more than another paying customer at the fights.

But you don't come from a family of fighters without developing a certain doggedness in the face of adversity. No nephew of Joe Monte was going to be pushed around by some political hack that knew nothing about boxing. Not this one, anyhow. I was determined to go the distance with the bureaucracy or go down swinging.

By now America was fighting in Korea, Eisenhower was elected President and *I Love Lucy* had become a hit on early network television while I waited to catch my big break. Finally, there appeared to be a ray of light at the end of the tunnel. Robert Christenberry retired as chairman of the NYSAC, and his successor was Judge Julius Helfand. That seemed like a propitious change to me and represented what was certainly a last chance, but still a chance, to make my dream come true.

Helfand, I reasoned, was an educated man. Moreover, he was a judge and judges, after all, are supposed to administer justice. All I needed, I thought, was a hearing and the plain truth of my situation would be clear to the new chairman.

So every day I made it a point to visit Judge Helfand's office, and every day his secretary, Mrs. Bowden, a big blustery sentry, would inform me, in a tone that would never be construed as apologetic, that Judge Helfand was unavailable. This ritual between us went on interminably as I refused to be discouraged. Soon, Mrs. Bowden developed a genuine dislike for me. Frankly, she did nothing for my appetite, either.

Ours was a game I soon tired of playing. I came to believe that Mrs. Bowden was deliberately keeping me from seeing the judge. Something had to give—the last few weeks had been miserable. I was growing surly, and my usual optimism became shrouded with anger and frustration. This bellicose gatekeeper had made me restless and embittered. I found myself unable to sleep, to concentrate, to work. I resolved this had gone on long enough and that the next day, Mrs. Bowden or no Mrs. Bowden, I was going to get an audience with the judge.

The next morning I presented myself to the NYSAC and asked to see Judge Helfand yet again. Snorting like the bull elephant that she was, Mrs. Bowden, as usual, brusquely dismissed me with her rote "unavailable" speech. But this time, I rewrote the script. With a move right out of Gale Sayers's playbook, I faked walking out and made a sharp left turn around her desk and, with resume in hand, I headed straight to Judge Helfand's closed door.

I can still hear the horrified shrieking that trailed me: "Young man! Young man! Where do you think you are going?" As if she didn't know.

I burst into the judge's office and began talking as fast as I could. "Judge, I am terribly sorry for this intrusion, sir, but I have been trying to see you for weeks about getting my license as a boxing referee, and if you will just look at my qualifications—"

At that point a fully enraged Mrs. Bowden arrived, bellowing, on the scene, voicing apologies to the judge and complaining bitterly about the insolence of "this young man."

As we both tried to talk over one another, the judge, with an imperial wave of his hand, silenced us. Then, for what seemed like an eternity, he sat there reading my resume. Clearing his throat at last, the judge rendered his decision. "All right," he said, "I will talk privately with Mr. Mercante."

Her hopes for the death penalty dashed, Mrs. Bowden left—but not before she threw me a look that, for sheer balefulness, would have given Sonny Liston the chills.

"Mr. Mercante," Judge Helfand said when we were alone, "I can see you're eminently qualified. But it takes more than qualifications and experience to get your license. You're still young, so let me give you a piece of fatherly advice. In this world you need friends, and friends in high places don't hurt anyone's ambitions. So why don't you get with the program and stop pushing doors that are marked 'pull.' If you follow the rules, I'll guarantee that not only will you get your license but with your background you will be doing main events before you know it."

The judge concluded our little class in Political Science 101 by advising me to see a Mr. Kane at the Democratic Club on Prospect Avenue and, as he put it, make myself useful. Political involvement was a good thing. So was hurrying past Mrs. Bowden without so much as a sidelong glance.

chapter 4

THE BLOCKBUSTER & GLORIA

T HROUGHOUT THESE YEARS I remained a carefree bachelor and, I must confess, enjoyed every minute of it. I had an apartment at the Merchant Marine Academy and on Sundays came home for a taste of family life, which was a refreshing respite from my frenetic lifestyle.

While I experienced hardly a dull moment, I felt there was something incomplete about my bachelorhood. I had to admit that I found something deeply appealing about home life and family. The variety and spontaneity that comes with having no commitments was a poor substitute for caring for someone and having someone care about you.

I met Gloria Oggiano while doing charitable work for the Heart Association Fund at the Waldorf-Astoria. She was charming, attractive and sweet-natured. I was immediately drawn to her and wasted no time in asking her out. But where do I take her on our first date? A movie, perhaps? A walk along the beach would be nice, or maybe a romantic candlelight dinner. No—this called for something really special. Something like—well, what better than a night at the fights! Gloria knew nothing about boxing and seemed a little hesitant. But I told her we were not going to just any old boxing match. That wouldn't do for a girl like her. This match would be for the Heavyweight Championship of the World!

That was how I convinced my future wife to go see the Rocky Marciano–Jersey Joe Walcott fight on our first date in September

1952. And what a battle royal it was, from its explosive beginning to its shattering climax in the thirteenth round when Marciano, bleeding, battered and trailing on all cards, backed Walcott into the ropes and landed the single greatest punch I ever saw. It was a short, compact, absolutely devastating right cross whose impact violently distorted Walcott's face into a grotesque mask, leaving the demolished champion swaying eerily and unconsciously on the ropes. As Jersey Joe snoozed like Rip Van Winkle, a new, dynamic champion was crowned king.

To my delight Gloria, gentle and feminine as she was, enjoyed every moment of this thrilling battle. Afterwards we went to a diner for a sandwich and coffee. We talked all evening and before we said goodnight I knew that nothing in my whole life would be more important than what was happening to me that evening, something that would change my life forever. I knew then that, as hard as Jersey Joe Walcott was hit, I was hit even harder—only mine was a paralyzing blow to the heart whose effects, I am happy to report, still haven't worn off.

While a torrential rainstorm roared outside, Gloria and I were married at the main altar at Saint Patrick's Cathedral. They say rain on your wedding day means good luck. It certainly was for me. We have had a fabulous marriage, one that has never lost its spark. Gloria blessed me with four wonderful sons of whom I am very proud. Though they are now grown, they all still love and adore their mother as I do, and always will.

Driving home after that first date with Gloria, I could not get over that my pal who hailed from my old hometown of Brockton, Massachusetts, was the new Heavyweight Champion of the World. Why, it was less than a year ago when, leaving the New York Athletic Club, I heard my name being called in that unmistakable southern New England accent. I turned to see the craggy face of the fighter they called the "Brockton Blockbuster." He had come down from his training camp at Grossinger's Resort and was hauling his own grips out of the trunk of his car.

Whenever I saw Rocky Marciano, I marveled over this squat heavy-weight's formidable muscularity. Fighters didn't lift weights then, and Nautilus machines were still years in the future. But believe me, they didn't call him the "Rock" because he was built like a pebble. He was the "Rock," with a physique that looked as if it had been chiseled in concrete. Physical conditioning and muscle tone were an important part of my own regimen, but next to Rocky I felt like Don Knotts before a good meal.

Marciano had recently signed to fight Harry "Kid" Matthews, with the winner to get a shot at the title. I wished Rocky luck. I could hardly believe he had made it so far. It seemed like yesterday when Rocky went to my uncle Joe Monte to see what Uncle Joe thought of his prospects as a pro. My uncle told him to forget it. At five foot ten inches tall, Rocky was too short for a heavyweight—the aver-age welterweight had a longer reach—and at twenty-three, almost twenty-four, Marciano was too old to be starting out. "Kid," my un-cle told him, "forget it. Fighters win championships before they're twenty-three."

Sounded like good advice. Fortunately, Rock didn't heed it. True, Rocky had some glaring physical disadvantages. But nature had en-dowed him with compensations: a cast-iron chin, enormous physical strength, and what columnist Red Smith described as "a right hand that registered nine on the Richter scale and a left hook that shook the upright like an aftershock."

I never met a more determined human being than Rocky Marciano; no fighter ever trained harder or sacrificed more in his quest to win and defend the heavyweight championship. His fights were wars and often he looked worse than the loser. Sometimes he took three or four punches to land just one of his own. Primitive—you bet. But this compact package of sheer guts, raw power and unbridled ferocity proved unbeatable. When his fists could not reach an opponent's chin, Rocky used his two sledgehammers to batter their arms, breaking blood vessels until they could no longer hold up their fists. I saw him do it to Roland LaStarza in their championship encounter.

There was a lot of inside talk that Rocky could have disposed of Rollie much earlier but, instead, punished the Bronx heavyweight for saying to the newspapers that a guy who takes as many punches as Rocky was bound to go punch drunk. The Rock didn't appreciate that. During the fight, the Brockton Blockbuster blockbusted LaStarza, with blows busting blood vessels in both arms, cracking ribs and fracturing his nose and jaw. Rollie was not a pretty sight and was never again half as good a fighter—in truth, the Rock ruined the kid.

The mega-tonnage in Rocky's fists was made all the more effective by the volume of punches he would throw in a fight. Rocky just never stopped punching and with his nearly superhuman endurance was able to fight the fifteenth round as if it were the first. Let me say this about the Rock: If it ever came down to a finish fight with any of his predecessors or successors, where determination and stamina were the deciding factors, my money would be on Rocky.

After the LaStarza championship bout, Rocky's come-from-behind victories against Ezzard Charles, twice, and Archie Moore became the stuff of legend. But Rocky had no intention of making Roland LaStarza a fortune-teller. Unlike most champions, Marciano knew when to hang up the gloves, and when he did, nothing could entice him to put them back on again. His unmatched record says it all: 49 fights, 49 victories, 43 by knockout—the only heavyweight champion to retire undefeated.

Rocky and I had a lot in common: born in Brockton; sons of Italian immigrants who worked in shoe factories; and, of course, we both loved sports, though Rocky's youthful ambitions focused more on the baseball diamond than the boxing ring. Things were tough back then, money scarce. But Rocky seemed more affected than most of us by his humble beginnings. He was a true son of the Depression; the deprivation of his childhood made him a great fighter, but it also left lifelong scars. The only fear Rock ever had was of going broke, and as a result he developed a deep-seated parsimony and an almost paranoiac suspicion of being taken advantage of in business dealings. I learned about this firsthand after Rocky's retirement from boxing when the subject of money caused a rift between us that was never bridged.

When I worked for Rheingold Breweries as deputy director of public relations, I worked with Frank Delano, the account executive for Foote, Cone and Belding, a prestigious advertising firm representing Rheingold. Delano was a distant cousin to President Franklin Delano Roosevelt and had the air and breeding of a true aristocrat. Tall, stately, impeccably dressed, Delano had the same podium-pitched voice of the former president. In the early 1960s, I was organizing the Rheingold-sponsored Monday Night Fights. I had arranged that former sports columnist Jimmy Powers would be broadcasting the televised fights. I told Delano that it would be a good promotional idea to have a former boxing champion work alongside Powers as co-analyst. In fact, each week we could invite a different champion to share the microphone with Powers.

"I think that's a great idea," Delano said. "But who would we get?"

"Well," I answered, "why don't we get Rocky Marciano and start the show off with a real bang? You can't believe how popular this guy is with the fans. Why, the Rock can't even walk through the airport or a crowded street without being mobbed by autograph seekers. The fans love him and he's more popular now than when he was champ."

"Do you think you can get him?" Delano anxiously asked.

Was he kidding? Not only did Rocky and I have a personal history but also my father-in-law, a gifted portrait artist, had sculpted a beautiful bronze bust of him when he was the Heavyweight King. It was a magnificent piece of artwork that really impressed Rocky. The Rock always told me that if I ever needed him he was only a phone call away.

In the years following his retirement, Rocky was a far cry from the savagely hungry, blue-collar fighter he had once been. The athlete who was legendary for denying himself every creature comfort now lavished in all its excesses. All the trappings of the good life flowed freely about him and the once lean, granite-like physique had grown heavy and ponderous. Marciano, the Spartan, had surrendered to the temptations of the world.

I phoned Rocky as soon as I got back to my office, and I explained the whole setup. I told him he would have the honor of being the first of announcer Jimmy Powers's guest champions and talked about how this would be good for boxing and good for him. His first question jarred me like one of his howitzer body blows.

"How much, Art?"

"What's that, Rock?"

"I said, Art, how much are these guys paying me?"

"Well, Rocky, I presume they will be paying scale."

There was a prolonged lull on the other end of the line. "Rock, are you there?" I asked tentatively.

"Scale, Arthur? Are you telling me they want me to appear as a guest commentator on television and they are paying me scale? You got to be kidding me."

"Well, Rock, that's what they pay. I'm sure if I talk to them they can do a little better."

"A little better," the Rock said incredulously. "A little better. Art, I'm your *paison*, the undefeated Champion of the World, and you're telling me maybe they could do a little better. That's bullshit, Art, and you know it."

"Rock," I said, trying to tone things down, "you're taking this much too personally. I'm just trying to put a program together."

But there was no reasoning with him. I had touched a raw nerve—his wallet. Marciano's competitive instincts were fully aroused, and I felt like Jersey Joe Walcott must've felt that night in Philadelphia Municipal Stadium: the Rock kept coming and there was nothing I could do to stop him from lowering the boom.

"You know, Art, when I was fighting, those television big shots really made the dough off of us fighters, and they're still doing it and I'm just not going to take it anymore," he railed.

I could see this conversation was going nowhere fast, but before I could say anything else, the champ hung up on me. Normally, the Rock was soft-spoken, good-natured, puppy-dog friendly, the exact opposite of his brawling roughhouse style in the ring. But when money was involved, especially if he thought he was getting screwed, he became angry, hostile and sometimes dangerous.

For a few minutes I just sat there numbly in my office. I had promised Rocky Marciano and I had failed miserably. Now what?

It was time to consider other options, and fast. Marciano, I figured, wasn't the only big name in boxing. What about Jack Dempsey? After all these years, the Dempsey name was still magic.

I had become friendly with Jack after we worked together in the movie *Requiem for a Heavyweight,* and I decided it wouldn't hurt to pay him a call at his restaurant. Jack Dempsey's, located on Broadway and Fiftieth Street in New York City, was a great landmark for sports writers and fans alike. The Manassa Mauler readily agreed to my proposal.

"If it's good for boxing, I'd be delighted to do it," Jack told me. "And you don't even have to pay me." After we shook hands I decided there wasn't a bigger Jack Dempsey fan than me.

The telecast couldn't have gone better. Jim Powers and Jack Dempsey were of the same generation so it was great entertainment hearing both of them reminisce about old times. Ratings went up steadily and having former champions on the broadcast became a highlight of the show.

Not long after that first telecast, I received a phone call. It was Rocky Marciano. His tone had completely changed; now he spoke softly, almost apologetically: "Gee, Arthur, I saw Dempsey working the broadcast of the fight. It really came out great and, ah—I changed my mind; I would really like to do one of the shows."

"Can't help you, Rock," I replied coldly. "We've already booked a boxing celebrity for every show."

Rocky, as was his wont in the ring, persisted: "I'm sure, Arthur, there is some way you can get me on. I would really appreciate—"

"Sorry, Rock, we're booked," I interjected, with a severity and abruptness that surprised me. After all, he was Rocky Marciano. We were both very upset. We never spoke again.

Over the next few years I would occasionally see Rocky at championship fights, a boxing awards dinner or sometimes dining at Vesuvio's on West Forty-seventh Street with Bernie Castro, owner of Castro Convertibles. We would glance over at one another but never offered a greeting. It was uncomfortable as hell. In fact, I really thought the whole thing had become ridiculous and that we should just shake hands and forget about it. But pride got in the way. I could not, in spite of myself, make the first overture; and neither, apparently, could Rocky.

Labor Day morning 1969 had dawned hot and muggy when I began my daily regimen of exercise and heard a bulletin over the radio: Former undefeated Heavyweight Champion Rocky Marciano and two companions had been killed in a small plane crash the evening before. The pilot had attempted a forced landing when the light aircraft struck a lone oak tree in the middle of an Iowa cornfield.

I was too stunned to think. Appalled and heartsick, I read the morning newspaper accounts with growing horror, agonizing over our little feud that ended a warm friendship. Now looking back, it all seemed so ridiculous, so foolish.

One newspaper wrote of the plane crash that it had to be something big—really big to stop the Rock. That's how I felt; he seemed so indestructible. It was a lonely time for me as I pondered my own mortality, a lost friendship and the folly of false pride.

But as time went by I made my peace with it. As is so often the case, the Rock's greatness as a fighter was even more appreciated after he was gone. As long as men cherish courage and a fighting spirit, the Rocky Marciano story will endure in the annals of sports. As an Italian-American and a kid from the old neighborhood, I'm proud to have seen Rocky take his rightful place in the pantheon of ring immortals, for no champion ever wore the heavyweight crown with greater dignity, nor graced it with more valor than this son of an Italian shoemaker.

chapter 5
BREAKING IN

O N MARCH 21, 1954, my dream of being a professional boxing referee was finally realized when I refereed a preliminary bout between heavyweights Wayne Bethea and Joe Rowan.

I can't recall a thing about the fight, including even who won. But I do recall being thrilled about the $50 I received for my services that night. It must have been a satisfactory debut because I began getting assignments on a regular basis, and by 1955 I was refereeing main events.

Officiating these fights was a great experience, and the extra pocket money that came from refereeing was especially welcome when I learned Gloria was pregnant with our first child. In those days the standard fee for refereeing a fight was $40, although you could make as much as $50 on a good night. That extra $10 made a real difference. And then came the day in January 1957, when I refereed the semi-final bout before the first Sugar Ray Robinson–Gene Fullmer middleweight championship fight. I was paid an eye-popping $175! I thought I was rich.

Refereeing might look easy when watching it on television, but in reality it is quite demanding, both physically and psychologically. The action is constant for three minutes a round, anything can happen at any time and you need to know how to control the fighters and keep an eye on what's going on in the corners between rounds. You need to be firm, but never intrusive; alert, but not overreactive; mobile, but never out of position to intervene at a moment's notice. You can never get caught up in the emotions of the crowd; you need to be your own judge and jury, with confidence enough to trust in your own judgment.

I found the transition from refereeing the amateurs to the professional ranks easier than I thought. In the pros, the fighters were usually more skilled, knew how to clinch and the rules were not as stringent. There was, of course, the adjustment of going more than the standard three rounds in the amateurs, but I was in good shape and learned something new with every fight.

The 1950s were a good time to break into professional boxing, which underwent something of a rebirth thanks to a new craze called television. Boxing matches actually began to be televised in 1944, but back then almost no one had a television set in his home. When I began refereeing professionally ten years later, nearly everyone had one. At the time, everybody agreed that boxing and television seemed like a marriage made in heaven. In the early days of television, the athletes in team sports such as baseball and football, with their huge playing fields, looked like ants on those small televisions. But boxing filled the screen.

There were fights on television every night of the week except Sunday. Boxing, like Jehovah, rested on the seventh day. Ultimately, with so many fights being broadcast, boxing would die of overexposure; but for a number of years the sport thrived. Through the prism of the '50s, the only apparent downside of this new technology—and it was a big one—was that it killed off the small fight clubs. Fans stopped going out to watch boxing after it was available for free right in their living rooms. The upside was that it gave promising young fighters a notoriety that would have been impossible in the pre-television age. So, along with Uncle Miltie, Sid Caeser and Imogene Coca, Gleason and Carney, and Lucy and Desi, boxers became the earliest stars of the new medium.

Television magically transformed your easy chair into a ringside seat where you could cheer on your favorite fighters. There were colorful guys like the great Kid Gavilan, with his famed bolo punch, and "Golden Boy" Art Aragon from the West Coast; and stalwarts like Ralph "Tiger" Jones, who I swear was the victim of more lousy decisions than any boxer I ever knew. There was Joey Giardello from Philadelphia, who never got his just due but fought all the great young black fighters most other white fighters avoided like they were food poisoning.

Television showcased matinee-type fighters: fighters like the collegially bred Chuck Davey and Chico Vejar, whose boyish looks stood out in stark contrast to the mashed noses and cauliflower ears of some grizzled performers. There were also the two-fisted, non-stop battlers like Gil Turner and Ernie Durando, and so many more.

In those years, I refereed fights featuring Rory Calhoun, Danny Giovanelli, Ludwig Lightburn, Tony Anthony, the boxer-puncher Rocky Castellani, Frankie Ryff and an Argentinean middleweight named Eduardo Lausse, who could literally kill you with his left hook. I also remember the talented Charlie Cotton and the underrated Vince Martinez. I'll never forget Holly Mims, who could fight off the ropes just as well as anyone, including the canny Archie Moore or Muhammad Ali during his rope-a-dope performances.

Some of the young fighters I refereed went on to become world champions, leaving me with a sort of "I knew them when" feeling. I can see them in the ring now, as if it were just yesterday: Harold Johnson, Willie Pastrano, Emile Griffith, Benny Paret, José Torres, Dick Tiger and Denny Moyer. I remember a terrific battle I refereed between two great lightweights, Carlos Ortiz and Johnny Busso. Ortiz, the winner, became the Lightweight Champion of the World. Busso was nearly as good, but he ended up one of the many undeservedly forgotten fighters of the ring. Boxing, like life, can be fickle and cruel.

As these young fighters learned and honed their skills in the 1950s, I improved mine as a referee. Nothing teaches like experience, and I was getting plenty of it in classrooms like Ridgewood Grove, Saint Nick's Arena, Eastern Parkway (popularly known as the "House of Upsets") and Sunnyside Gardens. All of America became familiar with these venues and also with the announcers who called the matches held there. Ted Husing was a real pro and so was Russ Hodges, who immortalized "The Giants won the Pennant! The Giants won the Pennant!" (perhaps the most famous call in sports history), and later there was Long Jack Drees and the smooth-talking Don Dunphy, who was already famous as the blow-by-blow announcer on radio—all of them now became known to millions of television viewers. Even the ancient George Bannon, who had been timing rounds since the turn of the century, became, with his signature duckbill cap, a celebrity in his own right.

Boxing on television not only helped careers, it was also a boon to the companies that sponsored it to sell Gillette razor blades, El Producto cigars, Mennen after-shave and, of course, Pabst Blue Ribbon Beer. A lot of people and products were benefiting from all those boxing telecasts.

I certainly wasn't left behind. Thanks to TV, my work in the ring was widely noticed and favorably commented upon. Some observers were kind enough to refer to me as the best young referee in the business. I don't know about that, but I do know that my appearances on television refereeing these fights caused quite a buzz in my little neighborhood. People were always stopping me on the street to say they had seen me on television last night. They got quite a kick out of it and, for that matter, so did I. Nobody was confusing me with Tyrone Power, but I had my share of admirers.

You must remember that in 1955, television was relatively new and still very much looked upon as a small technological miracle. Back then, there were only three major networks and, unlike today's bonanza of around-the-clock programming, television was only on during the prime hours of the day and evening. So to appear on this magical tube was quite an extraordinary occurrence.

As I look back at those early years of my career, I am deeply grateful for my good fortune. Of course, like any young, ambitious referee, I was itching to get assigned to my first championship bout. After I watched the Archie Moore–Yvon Durelle light heavyweight title fight in 1958, that ambition burned hotter than ever.

To this day, Moore–Durelle I remains my all-time favorite fight and, if it were mine to choose, the fight I would most love to have refereed. As it turned out, it was one of my boyhood idols, former Heavyweight Champion Jack Sharkey, who drew the assignment.

The emotion and drama of Ancient Archie coming off the canvas three times in the first round, and again in the fifth round, only to miraculously KO Durelle in the eleventh round epitomized, for me, the very essence of what we call "heart" in boxing. I longed for the day when I, too, would referee a history-making title fight.

I had no way of knowing then, of course, that with the dawning of the 1960s, my career as a championship referee was about to begin, and I would end up refereeing more championship fights than any other referee in boxing history.

chapter 6

JOSÉ TORRES, RHEINGOLD BEER & ME

O N THE NIGHT of October 13, 1958, a young, dynamic fighter from Puerto Rico named José Torres fought at St. Nicholas Arena. On a real good night, Saint Nick's normally attracted about 1,800 spectators; but on this evening the crowd was overflowing with more than 2,500 fans, most of them Latino. Hundreds more were turned away at the door. Clearly, a big new star was rising in boxing's firmament. I knew Torres was popular, but I was not prepared for the outpouring of unabashed adulation his fans showered upon him. I had never seen anything like it.

A member of the 1956 U.S. Olympic team, Torres won his seventh pro fight when he stopped Frankie Anselm in the ninth round that evening. As I raised Torres's right arm in victory, the overflow crowd erupted in wild celebration. José's delirious fans couldn't get enough of their hero and appeared to be getting ready to storm the ring. With security being sparse and so much raw emotion and national pride rising dangerously to flood tide, I honestly feared we were going to be trampled at ringside.

Just as a stampede looked imminent, José Torres calmly walked up to announcer Johnny Addie and politely asked for the microphone. Getting it, Torres, with the poise of a seasoned politician, quieted the crowd and began to speak.

The boxer made a strong and emotional appeal for everyone to be obedient and respectful citizens in the great city of New York. When he finished speaking the crowd gave him a standing ovation and filed out peacefully. You could not help but be tremendously impressed by this sensational young fighter and his message of civic responsibility and good citizenship. It was an eye-opener for me; I could not help thinking that this was the ideal spokesman Rheingold Breweries had been searching for.

In 1958, I was the deputy of public relations for Rheingold Breweries, Inc. At that time, Rheingold was the number-one selling beer in New York. But our hold on the market was slipping as sales gradually declined in the Hispanic market, a development causing considerable anxiety among Rheingold's top brass. Did Mercante have any ideas on how we might shore up this end of the market? I pledged to give the matter my utmost attention, and that night in musty Saint Nick's Arena, I thought I had found the answer.

The next morning I made an appointment to see the president of Rheingold, Philip Liebmann. I told him about José Torres and his legion of adoring fans. I proposed that Torres become the centerpiece of our promotional campaign for the Hispanic market. Liebmann thought the idea was worth trying and said I was not to waste any time in signing up Torres to be a player on the Rheingold team.

I hired José that very day and explained to him how he would function with our salesmen to promote the Rheingold product. He couldn't have been more cooperative and helpful. To kick off the campaign, we planned to have a ribbon-cutting ceremony in Spanish Harlem for one of our new breweries. Everything had been painstakingly arranged to make it a real public relations extravaganza guaranteed to make Rheingold the talk of the town. There would be lots of public officials on hand to wish the business well, and now we had Mr. Charisma himself, the hottest boxer in New York, who happened to be Puerto Rican, to gild the lily.

The morning dawned bright and beautiful, and everything went off without a hitch but for one Mack Truck–sized detail: José Torres was a no-show. At first I thought he was just late—but then the minutes and finally the hours melted away. My concern morphed into panic when no one could locate him. My great idea now resembled a public relations Hindenburg going down in flames.

Over the next several days I must have made two hundred phone calls to friends of Torres, boxing people, the police and every hospital in the metropolitan area. Not a sign of him, not even a clue. He had simply vanished. To make matters worse, every morning Liebmann was on the phone, asking if I had our missing headliner. "Not yet, sir," I would sheepishly reply, wishing I could instantly join Torres down whatever rabbit hole he had disappeared into.

Some three weeks later I sat mournfully sipping my morning coffee, trying to think of a way to resurrect my career at Rheingold, when, to my utter disbelief, José Torres casually walked into our sales office. It was August, and he was wearing a white Panama hat, a flannel shirt, and a pair of white slacks and shoes. He was totally relaxed and appeared not to have a worry in the world.

Smiling broadly, he greeted me: "Arthur Mercante, *Como esta amigo?*"

When I finally revived my senses, I incredulously replied, "What do you mean, '*Como esta amigo*'? Where the hell have you been?" My face was flushed; I bristled with indignation. "Do you have any idea of the grief, aggravation and embarrassment you have caused me?"

Caught off-guard by my reaction, Torres started to cover up as if I had just hit him with a stinging combination. Stuttering and stammering, he was looking to clinch and then he said that he had to go to Puerto Rico to visit his father, who was seriously ill. "Family comes first," he said, punctuating his sentence as if responding to me with a hard stiff jab.

I parried the blow and countered with some heat of my own. "It comes first with me, too, José, but after I made a commitment to someone I would have at least extended the courtesy of a phone call explaining why I was unable to fulfill that promise."

Torres looked defenseless; if this was a bout I would have mercifully stopped it. Lamely, he explained that he didn't have my phone number and added that he was so upset over his father's condition, he wasn't thinking straight. He apologized profusely and said he hoped he would be given the chance to make things right. I told him I would see what I could do.

I explained to Liebmann what happened, and soon we had Torres hooked up with some of our successful Hispanic salesmen. Things started humming along nicely, and sales of Rheingold in our targeted areas began to increase. With profits booming, the missed ribbon-cutting ceremony had become ancient history.

Everything was going great until one night, while driving in the Red Hook section of Brooklyn, I caught sight of a giant billboard advertisement that almost caused me to veer out of control. Pulling over for a better look, I got out of the car and stood there staring blankly in total, numbed, shell-shocked disbelief.

Towering about fifty feet above the pavement was a humongous billboard with a color picture of a beaming José Torres, holding a foaming glass of Schaefer beer. Underneath, in giant letters, was the tag line: *José Torres bebe cerveza Schaefer.* ("José Torres drinks Schaefer beer.")

I was aghast; I felt betrayed all over again, taken advantage of. I had bent over backwards to repair the damage from his "Invisible Man" impersonation and get him the best compensatory package possible, and this was the thanks I got—sleeping with the enemy! What a kick in the ass. The next morning I called José and told him to come see me at the brewery immediately.

When it came to chutzpah, José was in a pound-for-pound class by himself. When I demanded to know what possessed him to double-deal me and Rheingold like that, he blithely explained that he had received a nice sum from Schaefer and, besides, he didn't think there was anything wrong with endorsing two beers, anyway.

Looking at him intently, I said, very calmly and deliberately, "You don't think there is anything wrong with that, José?" As a matter of fact, no, he told me. "You don't see any conflict of interest there?" I pressed. No, he said, he really didn't, and as far as he was concerned there was nothing further to say on the matter.

I begged to disagree on that last point. There was, in fact, one more thing that needed to be said.

"Like what?" wondered José.

"Like, you're fired!" I shot back.

The episode with our two-fisted, two-brand future light heavyweight champion became the talk of both boxing and the breweries. When people asked me about it, I was honest: "Well, I hired him, and I fired him. And that's all there is to it."

In truth, José Torres was a terrific fighter and a legitimate idol to his countrymen. But dealing with him on a business level was enough to drive a man to drink—and I mean something a hell of a lot stronger than beer: Schaefer *or* Rheingold!

chapter 7

IN THE SPOTLIGHT OF HISTORY:
Patterson–Johansson II

T HE ROAR of the crowd, that's what I remember most—that thunderous, reverberating, cacophonous din. It was the loudest, most sustained sound I ever heard. All of Yankee Stadium seemed to be jarred by the earsplitting noise that pierced the night air that evening of June 26, 1959.

I managed to push my way to the radio broadcast table against the crush of the crowd. All I wanted was a tall, cold glass of ice water to soothe my parched throat, and in my haste I haphazardly crashed into a paying customer, spilling half the glass on him. To my amazement, glaring down at me was none other than the movie actor John Wayne. The Duke was making a movie with William Holden called *The Horse Soldiers,* and they had come to see the fight together. The look on his face told me this was no time to ask for an autograph.

Somehow, amid this suffocating mass of humanity, I espied Jack Duberstein, deputy commissioner of the NYSAC, frantically beckoning me from the other side of the ring. I switched directions and pushed my way over to him.

"Arthur," he screamed into my ear, "did you see those Johansson right hands? Did you see them?"

I wanted to say, "Yeah I saw them. Who do you think the timekeeper was? Who do you think was screaming the count over 19,000 hysterical fight fans as the Swedish challenger, Ingemar Johansson, smashed

Heavyweight Champion Floyd Patterson to the canvas—seven times in the third round!" After each knockdown I had to bellow at the very top of my lungs so that referee Ruby Goldstein could pick up the count.

I wanted to say all of this to Jack, but I was so hoarse I couldn't make a sound. Swallowing painfully, all I could do was nod once again and acknowledge, to my amazement, that the dimple-chinned Swede had become the first non-American since Primo Carnera to win the title.

Little did I know then how Floyd Patterson, Ingemar Johansson and Jack Duberstein would dramatically change the course of my career and, for that matter, my life.

Almost a year later, unbeknownst to me, Melvin Krulewich, the imposing chairman of the NYSAC, presided over a round-table meeting regarding the subject of ring officials for the Patterson–Johansson rematch. Jack Duberstein, who was in attendance, enjoyed regaling me for years afterward with the details of that little get-together.

Chairman Krulewich was addressed by everyone as "General," a rank he had held in the Marine Corps. He brooked no nonsense and conducted business at the NYSAC as if it were a divisional staff meeting. When the question of who would referee the fight came up, Duberstein suggested me. He had been trying to get me a headline fight for months but his efforts had been routinely frustrated.

"Arthur Mercante?" the General said, sitting in an exaggerated upright position. "Why, we need someone older, more experienced, to do this fight!"

"Well, General," Jack persisted, "Arthur has been doing fights for years at Saint Nick's and Eastern Parkway and—"

But Krulewich cut him off. "No, no, Jack. This fight is of great international importance. It is the fight of the year, and we can't just hand over this responsibility to some youngster. We need a referee with the status of a Goldstein or an Al Berl."

Jack dauntlessly pressed on: "General, excuse me, but Mercante did a masterful job in refereeing the Torres fight on the undercard of the first Patterson–Johansson, and he impressed everyone with how he took control of the Lausse–Pigou fight at Saint Nick's last week. That wasn't an easy fight to referee, you know."

"Look, Jack," answered Krulewich, "you don't have to sell me on Mercante. He is a great young referee; it's only his youth that is against him. He'll get his chance soon enough; he is just too young to do a fight of this magnitude."

Thoroughly exasperated, Duberstein then did something he thought he would never do, something no one ever dared to do to the General's face. He was downright—and loudly—insubordinate.

"With all due respect, sir, but goddammit, General, how old do you want the guy to be?"

The room froze. It was as if Moses had snapped back at the Burning Bush on Mount Horeb. Surprised and a little frightened by his own rashness, Jack gulped hard and in a suppliant tone added: "Well, General, he is, after all, forty years old."

"What!" exclaimed a stunned Krulewich. "You mean to tell me that young man is forty years old? I can't believe it!"

Right then and there, it was a done deal. I was the guy. Not that anyone told me about it. Even as I sat in the Polo Grounds the evening of June 20, 1960, watching the preliminaries to the Patterson–Johansson rematch, I had no clue that I had landed the big fight. All I had been told was to be at ringside for assignment. Once I heard that veteran Al Berl had been told the same thing, I figured I was out of the running. There was no way I was going to knock Berl out of the box.

While I sat perusing the fight card and wondering what prelim bout I was going to do, I felt a tap on my shoulder. I turned to see the smiling face of Jack Duberstein. "Suit up, Arthur," he said. "You got the main event."

"You mean Patterson–Johansson?" I asked, stunned.

"Yeah, Art—do you know of another main event?" Thrusting a piece of paper at me he said: "Here's your check for the fight."

I found myself staring at a $300 check made out to Al Berl. Puzzled, I said, "But Jack, this check is made out to Berl."

"Oh yeah, I almost forgot to tell you. Pay no attention to that. Berl's name is nothing but a red herring—you know, to keep the bloodhounds off the scent of the trail. We wanted to keep your assignment top secret. Just give the check to Berl after the fight, and he will cash it for you and give you the money. It's all arranged. Now c'mon, suit up—you don't have much time."

Walking to the dressing room I thought, *What is this, a C.I.A. operation?* Top secret . . . eleventh-hour disclosures . . . a check with disinformation on it; talk of bloodhounds, red herrings, throwing off the scent, false trails. For Christ sake, you would have thought Jack and the General were planning to re-invade Normandy rather than conduct a prizefight. Well, there was no time to think about that now; this was the big break I'd been waiting for, and nothing else really mattered. An hour later, I was in the ring to officiate my first heavyweight championship fight. Standing in there awaiting the introduction of the fighters, I could feel the electricity, the tension, the sheer anticipation, like I never had before.

Aside from the fever pitch excitement, the only other thing I plainly remember before the introduction of the fighters was Floyd Patterson's manager, Cus D'Amato, sitting in the audience wearing a black derby and staring right at me. He had been suspended by the NYSAC for machinations involving the promotional rights to Johansson, and as a result had been barred from Patterson's corner.

I remember thinking this would be the first time in Patterson's professional career that D'Amato would not be in his corner, and I wondered what kind of effect that would have on this sensitive and mercurial young man. I did not have to wait long for the answer.

Patterson came out of his corner and began punching at a furious clip—fast and hard punches loaded with TNT. Patterson meant business, and Johansson must have realized from the opening stanza that this was not the same fighter he fought a year earlier. It was a big round for Floyd, and it set the pace for the entire fight.

The second round provided Johansson with his only advantage when he landed a powerful overhand right to Patterson's suspect chin. I saw Patterson was badly shaken by the blow, and I waited to see if there would be a repeat of what happened last year. But Patterson remained upright, and Johansson, having been stung by Patterson's earlier punches, was hesitant to follow up. He never got another chance.

In the fifth round Patterson landed a big left hook that floored Johansson for a nine-count. Johansson rose, shaken and wide-eyed; you could smell the scent of fear. Patterson was after him, almost recklessly so. With fists blazing, the punches but a blur to the naked eye, Patterson pursued his prey with a vengeance. I don't think I ever saw a heavyweight who could fire off punches as rapidly as Patterson did in those early years—not Tyson, not Louis, maybe not even Ali.

Johansson was backpedaling from the furious onslaught, his arms flailing incoherently, like a man who just accidentally stumbled into a hive of angry bees. As he instinctively pulled his head back, Patterson hit him with as swift and sweeping and pulverizing a left hook as I ever saw. It landed with deadly precision on the point of Johansson's jaw, and the dimple-chinned Swede fell backward as if he had been shot.

Johansson lay unconscious on the canvas, capillaries bursting in his mouth, his left foot twitching sickeningly from the shock of the blow. I tolled off a ten-count that, in retrospect, was a ludicrous formality. Johansson was out cold before he hit the floor—he was not getting up anytime soon. But back then the unspoken commandment was that you always gave the champion every consideration, and that included the full count. Not everything about the good old days was so good or so wise. As I removed Johansson's mouthpiece, rivulets of blood ran down from the corners of his mouth. Before or since I never, thank God, have been associated with a more violent knockout.

I motioned for help and instantly Johansson's handlers and two ringside physicians surrounded us. I looked on helplessly, dreadfully worried about Johansson's condition and thinking how ironic it would be if I finally got my turn in the national spotlight only to have a guy get killed on my watch. I wasn't the only one. Suddenly, as only he could do, broadcaster Howard Cosell insinuated himself in the middle of the maelstrom.

"Is he dead? Is he dead, Whitey?" hollered Cosell at Whitey Bimstein, Johansson's legendary trainer.

"No," Bimstein hollered back, "but the son of a bitch should be. I told him to watch out for the left hook!"

With an involuntary shudder, I walked away from the sensitive Bimstein and the shy and retiring Cosell. What I never walked away from that fateful night was the unpleasant understanding that regardless of one's preparation, knowledge and skill in refereeing, things can happen incredibly fast in the ring, and when they do you are powerless to do anything but count. In my entire professional career I never learned a more valuable and humbling lesson.

To everybody's great relief, Johansson was revived and left the ring under his own power. What could have been a nightmarish ending turned out to be one of the most memorable moments of my professional life. Frankly, I could not have inaugurated my big-time career with a more auspicious event. The second Patterson–Johansson match was the most anticipated boxing event since the second Joe Louis–Billy Conn fight nearly a decade and a half earlier. It was also one of the few big fights that lived up to its billing: exciting all the way and ending with a spectacular knockout. Last but not least, with Patterson becoming the first man ever to regain the heavyweight title, it was a glorious and unprecedented moment in boxing history.

chapter 8

THE SWEETEST OF THEM ALL:
Sugar Ray Robinson

I N 1962 I HAD the privilege to be assigned to referee the Sugar Ray Robinson–Denny Moyer fight in Madison Square Garden. Robinson had defeated Moyer four months earlier, but it had been a close enough shave to warrant a rematch. Moyer was not just an opponent; indeed, he was something of a boxing prodigy. Three years earlier, at the tender age of nineteen, he lost a very close decision to then Welterweight Champion Don Jordan in a title bout in Portland.

As I watched Robinson limber up in his corner, chills ran up and down my spine. I had idolized him during the high glory days of his youth, when he was truly the sweetest of fighters. Now, here I was the third man in the ring, officiating his last appearance in the Mecca of boxing.

But I quickly pushed all such thoughts out of my mind. Sentiment, no matter how nostalgic, has no place in the mind of a referee. I had a job to do, and it was to enforce the rules and to be unshakably fair to both contestants. I always admired referee Ruby Goldstein for having the courage to cast the only ballot for Jersey Joe Walcott in his first title fight with Joe Louis, in which Walcott lost a controversial split decision to the legendary Brown Bomber. Like Goldstein, I was determined not to let a fighter's reputation influence my actions in the ring.

When the bell sounded for the first round, I noticed that Robinson, even at the advanced age of forty, ancient for a boxer, could still move with the grace and lightness of a dancer. I always thought if Nureyev had been a boxer, he would have moved around the ring like Robinson.

The fight was a good one, and there were moments when you could espy in Robinson faint glimpses of the ghost of his greatness. As the fight progressed, however, the fancy footwork faltered; the machine gun bursts of combination punching became more infrequent and, when executed, showed but a pale imitation of the speed and power he once possessed. As the rounds dragged on, Moyer's youth began to impose itself. After the final bell, I did not hesitate to cast my vote for Denny Moyer.

As I think back to the salad days of Sugar Ray Robinson, my memories are suffused with a golden glow, like the feeling you get when you see or experience something undeniably special. For me, watching Robinson was like seeing a true artist at work. But unlike Rembrandt or Raphael, his canvas was not set on an easel but secured upon a ring platform; and there, brushing lightly upon it with nimble feet and colored by fistic strokes of dazzling combinations, Robinson painted some of the great masterpieces in boxing history.

I first knew him as Walker Smith, when he was the sensation of the Inter-City Golden Gloves competition. Though not yet out of his teens, he awed me with his potential, and nothing that transpired in the decades that followed ever diminished that glowing first impression. His gifts were so abundant that, even at a time when boxing was rife with talent, his dominance was total.

As an amateur, he was undefeated in eighty-five fights, most of these victories coming by the knockout route. Turning pro, Robinson, now a tall, lithe welterweight, was so good that he would not infrequently fight some of the best middleweights, usually giving away a dozen or more pounds. In his first 132 fights, he was defeated only once, that by the redoubtable Jake LaMotta, the toughest middleweight I or anyone else ever saw. In that fight, LaMotta outweighed Robinson by an incredible 16½ pounds, a difference unheard of today in the lighter divisions. Robinson defeated LaMotta in their five other bouts, turning the trick four times while still a welterweight and the last time for the middleweight championship, when he stopped the seemingly indestructible LaMotta in the thirteenth round ending one of boxing's great rivalries.

Robinson would've added the light heavyweight title belt to his collection in 1952, but when he fought champion Joey Maxim in Yankee Stadium, it was at least 104 degrees in the ring, and Maxim outweighed him by more than fifteen pounds. Still he dominated Maxim in almost every round and fared better than Referee Ruby Goldstein, who collapsed after the tenth round from heat exhaustion and was replaced by Ray Miller. But Maxim wisely conserved his energy as Sugar Ray built up a seemingly insurmountable lead with an extravagant display of punching and footwork that had Maxim lagging two steps behind as Robinson glided around the ring.

But the oven-like temperature inside the ring began to take its toll. At the bell ending the thirteenth round, Robinson, the very picture of grace and athleticism, awkwardly fell to the canvas after missing a punch. Exhausted from the torrid heat and the demanding pace he had set, Robinson failed to answer the bell for the fourteenth round. Meteorology and not Maxim kept him from becoming a triple-champ.

After fighting for almost a decade and a half, Robinson retired for 2½ years to perform a different kind of footwork as a dancer under the Broadway lights. But, missing the excitement, Robinson returned to the ring at age thirty-four, and it was during this second phase of his career that Robinson would, occasionally, find himself on the losing end of a decision—which oftener than not, he would reverse in a rematch. Astonishingly, he won the middleweight title five times, and I, among many others, thought he beat tough-as-leather Gene Fullmer in their rubber match, a victory that would have made him, at age forty a five-time winner.

"Fullmer was a tough customer. Boxing writer Bert Sugar once noted that if boxing were football, Fullmer would be penalized ten yards in every round for unnecessary roughness. But in their second fight, Robinson cleaned up Fullmer's act with one of boxing's picture-perfect left hooks. When a still brain-fog-induced Fullmer got up and saw Robinson and his cornermen jumping around and celebrating, he turned to his manager, the inimitable Marv Jensen, and asked what happened. Jensen deadpanned: "The referee counted to eleven."

In his prime Sugar Ray Robinson was, without doubt, ringdom's most gifted performer or, as the popular cliché goes, "pound for pound" the greatest fighter I ever saw. Today, nearly sixty years after his heyday, I am amazed at how often I am approached by young fight fans who want to know about Sugar Ray. It happens everywhere I go.

One evening while attending a New York Knicks–Chicago Bulls basketball game at Madison Square Garden, I was asked by a young man "Mr. Mercante, how good was Sugar Ray Robinson?"

I looked him in the eye and said, "Son, let me tell you something. Sugar Ray Robinson was at least as gifted an athlete in his sport as Michael Jordan is in his."

His eyes lit up; he nodded knowingly and quietly walked away. Nothing more needed to be said.

chapter 9
LIGHTS, CAMERA—ACTION!

After the Floyd Patterson–Ingemar Johansson fight, I had the pleasant surprise of finding myself somewhat in demand. Not only people associated with boxing but also business people and even show biz types sought me out just to say hello, ask me a question about boxing or invite me to get involved in some enterprise of theirs. I didn't mind the attention, and with a growing family I welcomed new business opportunities.

One of the most enticing offers I received came from television personality David Susskind, who was president of Talent Associates, the producer of plays for the TV program *Playhouse 90*. Susskind asked me to come to his office to discuss a role in a boxing movie he was producing. The movie was adapted from a television production of Rod Serling's *Playhouse 90* script "Requiem for a Heavyweight." Serling was a former amateur boxer, and his story centered on a washed-up heavyweight contender who was totally adrift in a world not bordered by ropes and ring posts. I had seen the telecast, starring Jack Palance, and found it very moving.

The next afternoon I found myself ushered into Susskind's spacious office. There, behind an enormous mahogany desk, his white hair combed back in a semi-pompadour style, sat David Susskind. He looked immaculately groomed in a suit perfectly tailored to what appeared to be an athletic frame.

"Mr. Susskind," I said, extending my hand in greeting, "it's a pleasure to meet you."

Walking around his desk and clasping my hand firmly he said with
a distinct air of cheerfulness, "You know, you and I are going to be
working together very closely, so why don't we dispense with the for-
malities? You can call me David, and I'll call you Arthur."

"That suits me fine, David," I replied.

Susskind explained his plan to make a big screen version of
Playhouse 90's "Requiem for a Heavyweight" and said he wanted
me to play the role of a referee and also serve as technical advisor
for the boxing scenes. He told me he had already signed some big
Hollywood stars for the project, including Anthony Quinn for the lead
role of heavyweight Mountain Rivera, and Jackie Gleason and Mickey
Rooney as members of the supporting cast. Susskind told me about
budget concerns and some of the logistical problems involved in turning a TV production into a full-scale feature film. He was very bright,
very engaging. I liked him immediately and without hesitation agreed
to be involved.

Escorting me out of his office, Susskind stopped at the door and
pulled me close to him as if he was about to confide some dark secret.
"There is one more thing you need to know, Arthur, and it's critical to
the plot of the movie. You know Quinn plays the role of a washed-up
contender whom the greedy promoters are using as fodder for rising young talent. Well, I'm going for realism in this picture. I want
a real heavyweight contender to play the boxer giving Quinn his last
dreadful beating. In fact, I want someone who is going to be the next
Heavyweight Champion of the World. You know all the prospects . . .
do you think you can deliver him to me? I mean, I don't expect you to
answer right away. Take a little time to think about it but, ah—can you
have this guy, whoever he is, come to my office by say—ah—no later
than next week?"

I gulped hard and told him I would do my best.

Talk about pressure; fortunately, by the time I got back to my office I had someone in mind who I thought would be perfect for the part. I called Bill Faversham in Louisville, Kentucky. He headed a consortium of investors, many of them heirs to old Kentucky fortunes, sponsoring an up-and-coming professional fighter who had won a gold medal in the 1960 Rome Olympics—a fighter named Cassius Marcellus Clay.

Clay had impressed me as an amateur. But I became totally convinced of his future greatness when I watched him on television in his ninth professional bout against veteran Alex Miteff. I thought it was a bad match for Clay, who was just nineteen years old and whose 188 pounds were somewhat sparsely distributed over his nearly six-foot-three-inch frame. Though two inches shorter, Miteff was a powerfully built 210 pounds and, at age twenty-seven or twenty-eight he had competed against some top-shelf competition. He was not championship caliber, but the Argentine brawler was a tough hombre, hard to hurt and even harder to discourage. Even more ominously for Clay, he could bang some, especially to the body. That did not bode well for the comparatively frail-looking teenager from Louisville, whom I thought was being rushed too fast into the big time.

At the start of the bout Clay was blazing fast, faster than I ever thought he could be. He repeatedly stung Miteff with quicksilver combinations. But true to form, Miteff fought back hard, hurting Clay with some vicious body shots. Several times young Cassius visibly winced from the blows, and it appeared he would eventually wilt from Miteff's brutal body attack.

But it didn't happen. Despite being hurt, despite the twenty-two pound weight disadvantage, Clay fought back. That is not an easy thing to do, especially for a teenager with just eight fights under his belt facing an experienced, battle-hardened warhorse like Miteff. In the sixth round, Clay scored a sensational knockout. I knew then that one day this kid would be champ. Cassius not only had a world of talent, but he also possessed the intestinal fortitude of a true champion.

That was more than a year earlier. Since then Clay was still undefeated and had put on some twenty pounds of muscle. To go along with his marvelous physique, Cassius had movie star looks and a personality full of charm and fun. I knew he would be perfect for the part. It didn't take much to sell Faversham on the idea. It would be great exposure for Cassius, not to mention a few extra bucks to line his pockets and Faversham's too.

That Friday when I walked into Talent Associates, there, sitting comfortably on the sofa, was the young fighter they called the "Louisville Lip." Cassius was quiet and polite, evincing none of the braggadocio and theatrics that either entertained or infuriated boxing fans and accounted for the nickname hung on him by sportswriters. We spoke quietly while we waited, mostly about his next fight. Little did I know that this polite young man would one day be the most recognized person on the face of the Earth, passionately loved or rabidly hated, depending on one's perspective or politics.

When we were called into Susskind's office, the producer's eyes widened at the sight of Cassius. Dressed in a cream-colored suit, the young boxer's striking looks, physical grace and charismatic appeal were obvious, if not overwhelming. But strangely, Susskind seemed uncomfortable and reluctant to embrace the young heavyweight, explaining that he was interviewing several contenders, and he ended the interview making no promises. Susskind thanked Cassius for coming, and as the producer walked Clay to the door, he asked me to stay for a minute.

"So, what do you think?" I asked a little tentatively when we were alone.

"Jesus Christ, Arthur, why did you bring him? The part calls for a white guy!" blurted Susskind.

I was stunned, nearly speechless. "David," I retorted, "you did not say that. You said to bring you the guy who is going to be the next Heavyweight Champion of the World—and this is the guy. You said nothing about the guy being white, and what the hell does it really matter anyway? I may not be in the movie business, but I know this kid will be great for the part."

Susskind's features softened a bit. "You may be right," he said. "I have to admit, the guy really is magnificent looking." After another moment's consideration, Susskind said, "Well, I guess a little dramatic license here and there doesn't hurt, and it might even help."

With that tentative note of approval, I stepped out and breathed a long sigh of relief. Cassius Clay was hired.

Production on the movie began in two weeks. I arranged to get as many ex-fighters as possible to appear in the film. Jack Dempsey, Willie Pep, Barney Ross, Abe Simon, Tami Mauriello and more were hired for cameo appearances to lend a sense of cinema realism. I also helped choreograph all the fight scenes. It was a great experience for me, and it turned out that the addition of Cassius Clay to the cast was a boon to production in more ways than one. His gregarious, magnetic personality helped alleviate some of the tension on the set between Anthony Quinn and Jackie Gleason who, frankly, did not hit it off.

Both were enormously talented actors, but their gifts flowed through different and often conflicting channels. Gleason was a spontaneous genius, who needed no rehearsals and had the ability to memorize his lines in an eye-blink; Quinn, on the other hand, was a method actor, who would laboriously review his script and try to mentally visualize every nuance of his performance.

While Quinn was always early on the set, Gleason staggered into the studio late, often in his cups from a long night's carouse. Grabbing the script on his way to the dressing room, he began consuming, in large gulps, what seemed like a gallon of black coffee. In no time at all, Gleason was miraculously sobered up and ready to go. It was an Academy Award–winning performance in itself. Meanwhile, Quinn was sitting in a corner of the set, still visualizing and mumbling his lines to himself.

"Goddammit, Tony!" Gleason would bellow angrily. "We don't have all day. Now get off your ass, and let's get on with it."

Fortunately, Cassius Clay was a great tension reliever, and his antics on the set continually broke everybody up. Gleason had a specially designed chair with his well-known sobriquet, "The Great One," embroidered in gold lettering on the backrest. The problem was that every time he went to sit in it, the chair was already occupied by the young heavyweight who proclaimed himself to be "The Greatest."

"You're sitting in my chair, Cassius," Gleason would growl, actually more amused than annoyed by the youngster's chutzpah.

Cassius would point to the inscription on the back of the chair and indicate that it could only mean him.

"No," Gleason would remonstrate, "I'm 'The Great One'!"

Cassius would beg to differ, and to prove his claim he would recite all his knockout victims and then challenge Gleason to name anyone he had ever knocked out.

"You better listen to him, Jackie," I chided once. "Your record against heavyweight contenders is none too good."

Gleason, a good sport when the mood was on him, roared with laughter and said in that big voice of his: "You're so right, Arthur, you're so right!"

What we were talking about was something that happened to Jackie when he was working nightclubs in New Jersey back in the late 1930s. Gleason loved to tell the story himself. One night, in the middle of his comedy act, a heckler's barbs began to get on his nerves. Jackie was a rough fellow with a reputation for being pretty good with his dukes, and when the heckler kept it up, Gleason invited the heckler outside to discuss the matter. The heckler ended the discussion with one punch, knocking Jackie out cold. When he came to, Gleason found out that the heckler was none other than heavyweight contender, Two Ton Tony Galento, who would fight Joe Louis for the title a year later.

During the filming I became very friendly with Anthony Quinn. He was a large, rawboned man who loved boxing. He had been a fairly successful amateur boxer before realizing he didn't have the goods to make it in the pros. Turning to acting he had become a Hollywood legend, but there was nothing phony about the actor, who told me right off the bat to call him "Tony." Every afternoon we would have lunch at a little place on Fifty-seventh Street and Eleventh Avenue. Tony would go made up as poor Mountain Rivera and loved the way people gasped at the sight of his blackened eyes, butterfly stitches, puffed-up nose and cauliflower ears. Everyone thought he was just a broken-down pug who'd taken too many punches. No one pegged him as the great actor Anthony Quinn.

At the conclusion of the filming, Tony presented me with a beautiful Cartier scarf, silk on one side and wool on the other. I still have it today, and it brings back great memories of those times and the warm friendship we shared. As for *Requiem for a Heavyweight*, it was a critical success, and although it portrayed boxing at its worst, it was a great experience for me to work with such consummate actors and to introduce into their ranks a young fellow who was pretty good at entertaining in his own right and who would go on to make the whole world his stage.

Cassius and I were in the very opening scenes of the movie. I reffed the bout in which he pummeled poor "Mountain Rivera." Later on, after he won the heavyweight title and became Muhammad Ali, we would be involved together in several other productions that dwarfed anything Hollywood had to offer.

chapter 10
MY FAVORITE BOUTS:
a referee's choice

P ROBABLY THE MOST frequent question I am asked by boxing fans is "What is the greatest fight you ever refereed?" Even though I have refereed thousands of fights, the question is not as difficult to answer as one might imagine. It would have to be, of course, a championship bout, since the level of skill shown in these fights is generally greater than non-title bouts, and with so much more at stake, the excitement is greater.

Using this as a guideline, and placing the Ali–Frazier and Patterson–Johansson fights in their own separate category as historic events in boxing history, there are two fights that really stand out over the years.

The first was the 1960 welterweight championship bout between Champion Benny Paret and challenger Federico Thompson. This was the encore encounter between these two fighters after a tremendously exciting twelve-round draw one year earlier. Now, with the championship on the line, the rematch promised to be a classic.

Cuba's Paret was one of those fighters who always gave the fans their money's worth. He lived by a code—a code to fight until he could fight no more. When he was in the ring, it was nonstop action. He gave no quarter and asked for none. Paret was an enormously courageous fighter, in fact, too courageous for his own good. One year and four months after the Thompson fight, Paret would be killed from injuries defending his title against Emile Griffith.

Federico Thompson was a marvelously gifted, albeit rather reluctant warrior, who performed with consummate craftsmanship. Like Ray Robinson, Thompson put the "sweet" into the science of boxing. Federico could fight on the inside, he could fight on the outside, and he could move with balletic grace, feinting you silly or just plain boxing your ears off. If he just had a little more drive, a little more pop in his punches, he would not only have been champion but a great one at that.

While Thompson's pugilistic wizardry was something to behold, it was Paret's constant pressure and bulldog tenacity that won the day. Paret never gave Thompson any rest; but there were many intermittent moments where Thompson dazzled the crowd with a virtuoso performance of boxing skills. While Featherweight Champion Willie Pep was the purest boxer I ever saw, Thompson was a welcomed reminder that boxing genius had not gone the road of extinction.

Unfortunately for Thompson, at age thirty-three his legs could not match Paret's. Ten years younger, Paret pressed the fight, constantly forcing Thompson to backpedal. Moving backwards is a bigger strain on the legs than moving forward, and this began to tell on Thompson as the fight moved into the later rounds. It was Paret's tenacity that ultimately won over Federico's skill and technique, but only after what was a truly titanic struggle between boxing science and two-fisted determination.

The other fight that remains indelibly etched in my memory is the 1978 contest for the Junior Lightweight Championship of the World between Alfredo Escalera of Puerto Rico and the challenger, Alexis Arguello. It was the most brutal and bloody fight I ever refereed.

The wettest, too. During the ring announcer's introductions, it started to rain buckets. It was the heaviest downpour in Puerto Rico in years, and it continued almost without letup throughout the fight. The outdoor crowd at Lobule Stadium, Puerto Rico, was soaked to the skin, but I'd be surprised if anybody ran for cover because the excitement of this crimson and savage battle had them glued to their seats.

Escalera, known as the "Snake Man," scored early in the first round, stinging the Nicaraguan challenger with some sharp punches. But in the second round Arguello struck back, throwing a sneaky left hook that sent the Snake Man down for a count of eight. More angered than hurt, Escalera came up, throwing bombs.

In the third and fourth rounds, Arguello began to land hits more frequently. His razor-sharp punches opened cuts over both of Escalera's eyes, around his face and inside his mouth. The champion's corner could not stop the torrent of blood. Yet, despite the cuts, the pain, the punishment, Escalera fought back, rocking Arguello several times with overhand rights.

At the end of the sixth round, Escalera's face was liquid red, and I called the commission medic, Doctor Amaury Capella, to the champion's corner to assess Escalera's wounds. Rules vary from place to place on who has the final say to stop a fight. In this bout it was the doctor who ruled that the fight should continue.

In the seventh and eighth rounds, Arguello continued to hammer the champion. In desperation, Escalera started using roughhouse tactics. I warned Escalera to fight by the rules, and for my trouble I was lustily booed by the partisan crowd.

Alfredo fought back gamely despite his deteriorating condition, proving to all that he was a valiant and courageous champion. It became clear to me that Escalera intended to win or be carried out on his shield. Fighting back, Alfredo threw a tremendous left hook, catching Arguello under the right eye and opening a large gash that bled freely. As the homeland hero seemed to rejuvenate at the sight of his opponent's blood, his legion of supporters became frenzied with jubilant hysteria.

But Arguello also had the heart of a champion, and he fired back, reopening Escalera's facial wounds that once again began to leak blood everywhere. My shirt turned butcher red. I would have stopped the fight after the eleventh round, but again the doctor decided to let it continue. Amazingly, Escalera rallied in the twelfth round with a burst of punching that had Arguello covering up. Arguello's left eye was now bloody and swollen, and goblets of blood began spurting from his mouth. The ring had turned into a mutual slaughterhouse.

In the thirteenth round, the fight turned again as Arguello landed a series of punches that had the champion reeling. I stopped the action and sent each man to a neutral corner. The tom-toms that had been beating with an incessant, primitive cadence throughout the evening went silent. A hush fell over the whole stadium as the crowd waited to see what would happen next.

I motioned for the doctor to come to the ring apron for a closer look, and he finally agreed with me that the fight should be stopped. Over the anguished cries of Alfredo Escalera, I declared Alexis Arguello the new champion, and both fighters received a standing ovation from the sated, half-drowned customers.

The crowd swarmed both fighters in appreciation as I walked out of the ring unnoticed. I was happy to be alone in my dressing room instead of sharing quarters with the two fighters, as had been the arrangement until I issued a strong protest. Fistic battles of this magnitude, where both combatants put themselves at great risk, drain a referee both physically and emotionally; it would have been too much to be in the same room with the winner and loser, surrounded by jubilation and desolation. After such a stirring rollercoaster-of-a-contest, I needed to be away from the fray to catch my breath and be alone with my thoughts and emotions.

chapter 11
THE TRIALS AND TRIBULATIONS OF A REF

IN BOXING, as in life, truth is often stranger than fiction. Although I never had anything happen in one of my fights that was quite as bizarre as a parachute landing in the ring, as occurred in the second Riddick Bowe–Evander Holyfield fight, I have had my share of weird and wild happenings.

Take for instance when I refereed the James J. Beattie–Johnny Barrazza fight before a black-tie audience, as part of the centennial celebration at the Saratoga racetrack in 1963.

James J. Beattie's boxing career began in the most peculiar and unusual fashion. He had answered a newspaper advertisement placed by a wealthy restaurateur looking for a white heavyweight. The ad promised that in exchange for an investment of hard work and faith in his handlers, all the fighter's daily needs and training expenses would be taken care of on his road to fame and glory. It was a brainstorm that harkened back to the days of the great Jack Johnson, when some people found the idea of a black heavyweight champion so objectionable that a great crusade was launched to find the so-called Great White Hope. I thought the brainstorm was brain-dead right from birth.

Nevertheless dozens of big strong white guys answered the latest call, and after a tryout James J. Beattie from Minnesota was judged to have the best chance of making it in the professional ranks. His management proceeded to cautiously feed him the customary diet of stiffs while mounting a PR campaign worthy of a presidential candidate, which eventually resulted in a documentary airing in prime time on ABC-TV.

As I entered the ring that evening and set eyes on Beattie, my first impression was that he shouldn't be fighting, he should be playing for the New York Knicks. In his socks, this Paul Bunyan in boxing gloves stood over six feet eight inches tall.

Unfortunately for Beattie and his investors, his stature turned out to be the most impressive thing about him. Almost before the sound of the opening bell had died away, I could tell Beattie was not much of a fighter. His opponent, Johnny Barrazza, had only journeyman skills, but he was strong and proved to be a fairly potent body puncher. He also had no trouble getting inside Beattie's long reach and bulling him to the ropes. Then, with both hands, he waled the daylights out of Beattie's midsection.

Beattie either couldn't or just didn't know how to tie up his opponent. The giant redwood was being methodically chopped down, and I was becoming concerned about how much more he could take. Meanwhile, I was having a hell of a time keeping Beattie from falling out of the ring and into the press row. The Saratoga ring had only three strands of rope instead of the now-standard four. Most of Beattie's great height was in his long legs and the backs of his knees almost came up to the top rope. So whenever Barazza backed Beattie against the ropes I would grab the top strand with my right hand and would lift it up near Beattie's shoulder blades and simultaneously yank him back away from the ring apron—no easy task, since Beattie weighed around 240 pounds.

You won't find this maneuver anywhere in the rulebook, but if I hadn't attempted it Beattie would have been out of the ring more than he was in it.

The three-minute rounds began to feel more like thirty, and I thought my arm was going to come right out of its socket. I began to wonder which would give out first—Beattie's midsection or my right arm. Beattie's midsection lost. By the fifth round, James J. Beattie had totally wilted under the body barrage, and it was pointless to let the fight go on.

Beattie continued to pursue his boxing career until one too many beatings convinced him to find an easier line of work. He found it as an actor and went on to appear in several "B" cowboy movies and even appeared on the popular *Gunsmoke* television series. But his biggest role came when he played former Heavyweight Champion Jess Willard, the "Pottawatomie Giant," opposite the great actor James Earl Jones as a Jack Johnson clone, and became on celluloid what he could never achieve in life: the "Great White Hope."

Beattie wasn't the only tall guy I had trouble with. In fact, compared to my experience with heavyweight contender Ernie Terrell back in 1964, the Beattie fight was a taffy pull. Terrell was fighting Bob Foster, making his first of several forays into the heavyweight division. Foster, who would go on to become one of the greatest light heavyweight champions of all time, had the height but not the heft to deal with the real big guys. And Terrell was big, not only in terms of his six-foot-six-inch height but also his gargantuan wingspan. When Terrell stood at attention for the playing of the national anthem, I noticed that his gloves almost touched his ankles. It was his huge reach advantage that made Terrell troublesome for a lot of guys. Terrell's favorite weapons were a long left jab and a smothering bear hug.

The largely uneventful fight was mostly a one-sided affair with Terrell dishing out the punishment. In the fourth round the two fighters fell into one of their frequent clinches. Now, breaking a clinch may seem easy to the spectator at ringside or the television audience at home, but it can be a difficult, and even dangerous, task—especially when heavyweights are involved.

It is a situation in which the referee deliberately puts himself in harm's way. My refereeing style is to be as inconspicuous as possible.

When fighters clinch, however, you have no choice but to place your-self right in the middle of the action, or more accurately, the inaction. In separating the boxers I always make sure to push the fighters far enough away from each other so that no one gets hit on the break, in-cluding myself. But as I broke Terrell and Foster, I miscalculated, for-getting about Terrell's freakishly long reach. After I pushed them back to what I thought was a safe distance, Terrell instantly fired a long left hook that caught my chin at the end of its arc. If I had been any closer, the blow might have decapitated me.

The next thing I knew, Terrell was bouncing me up and down and apologizing profusely. I was in a haze, but fortunately the bell sounded the end of the round. I walked back to a neutral corner and looked on imploringly as the handlers administered smelling salts to the two fighters. Hell, I was the one who needed reviving, having absorbed the heaviest blow of the round. Unfortunately, there are no cornermen as-signed to help the referee.

Luckily, I was still young and in good shape, so that by the start of the fifth round I felt no ill effects except for a distinct loosening of my two front teeth. Terrell continued to dominate the fight, and by the seventh round he was repeatedly hitting a defenseless Foster and there was no reason to let it go any further. I stopped the fight and declared Terrell the winner by a TKO.

As the announcer proclaimed the time of the stoppage, I noticed Terrell moving menacingly toward me. It's not too unusual for the loser of a stopped fight to protest the referee's action, but for the win-ner to kick up a fuss would be totally bizarre. But that's what hap-pened. All of a sudden Terrell began swearing at me, shoving me and threatening to kick my ass. You'd have thought I was the one who had mistakenly punched him in the face.

Terrell was a big, scary looking guy, and just when it seemed like he was going to assault me right there in the ring, his manager, Julie

Isaacson, who was almost as big as Terrell, jumped in between us and demanded to know what the hell his fighter's problem was. According to Terrell, I had committed the cardinal sin of stopping the fight before he had a chance to stretch Foster out on the canvas for a clean knockout.

Even Isaacson was incredulous. "Knock him out! Knock him out?" he screamed at Terrell. "Why you big stiff, how were you going to knock out Foster when you couldn't even knock out this little referee with the best punch you ever threw!"

The towering Terrell looked down at me and then around at everyone within earshot of Isaacson's delicious putdown. Mortified, he sheepishly exited the ring without uttering another word.

Another tense moment came in 1982, when I refereed a televised fight between middleweights Mark Frazie and Dwight Walker that led me into a whole different kind of ambush. Throughout the fight Walker repeatedly hit Frazie below the belt. I issued several stern warnings and twice had points deducted for his infractions. But Walker continued throwing his submarine punches, and before the tenth and final round I warned him and his manager, Murad Muhammad, that one more low blow would give me no choice but to declare Frazie the winner on a disqualification.

So, no sooner does the tenth round begin than Walker throws a terrific uppercut whose destination was so south of the border, it needed a visa. When it landed, Frazie's trunks went up like a hot air balloon. Clearly the punch was deliberate, and I immediately disqualified Walker, whereupon both he and Murad Muhammad went ballistic.

In such situations it is always best just to walk away until everybody calms down. I moved to the far side of the ring, as far from Walker and Muhammad as possible, only to see, with disbelieving eyes, NBC broadcaster Ferdie Pacheco, known as the "Fight Doctor," making a line for me with both of them in tow. Walker was boiling mad and looked ready to hit someone—namely, yours truly. Being familiar with

Walker's punching style, I immediately regretted not wearing a protective cup underneath my trousers.

With the television cameras rolling, Pacheco asked me why Walker was disqualified. I explained that it was for Walker repeatedly hitting Frazie in the groin in spite of my frequent warnings. When Pacheco turned to Murad Muhammad for his reaction, the manager demonstrated that his English diction was as shaky as his understanding of the rules by screaming that there was no proscription in the rulebook against "hitting a man in the 'goin'."

I responded, "What in the world are you talking about? Of course it's a rule!"

As this ludicrous scene went out to a national TV audience, the ranting Murad and Walker crowded me like a couple of schoolyard toughs. But I wasn't intimidated by their bullying and calmly stood my ground, and they finally stomped away, muttering endearments about me under their breath. I certainly never courted controversy, but when it came I wasn't cowed or meek. I didn't appreciate the bad judgment that led Pacheco to put me in the middle of a potentially incendiary situation like that. I suppose he thought it was "good television," but to me it was just another incident, after too many of them had already occurred, of hitting below the belt.

chapter 12
DANGER AND INTRIGUE

T HERE IS SOMETHING about being associated with boxing that
makes people want to test you, even when you're not one of the
guys wearing shorts and boxing gloves. And it's not always by some
loud-mouth in a bar who thinks that taking a shot at a professional
fighter will win him real standing with the boys down at the plant.

I remember an incident which happened to me during my installation into the International Boxing Hall of Fame. One of the rituals
performed during the induction weekend is to have a plaster mold
of each inductee's fist made for posterity—sort of boxing's version of
sticking your hands in cement on the Hollywood "Walk of Fame."

As I was on the dais with my fist in a bucket of plaster, former World
Boxing Association Heavyweight Champion James "Bonecrusher"
Smith was observing the process up close. Also on the dais was an
old friend from my navy days who kept coaxing Bonecrusher, who
didn't get his nickname for powder-puff punches in the ring, to take
a shot at my midsection. Smith just smiled.

"No," said my friend, "go ahead—Arthur's got a gut of granite."

In fact, I had never neglected my abdomen in my daily workout
regimen, and my reward for the thousands of sit-ups and leg-lifts
and crunches was, if I do say so myself, a stomach the shape and envy
of men half my age and younger. It had been the target of more than
a few playful pokes by friends and curiosity seekers over the years.
But I was never the kind who went around urging people to take

their best shot. Especially people called "Bonecrusher"!

When my brave friend persisted up there on the stage, Smith tried to placate him by giving my stomach a tentative little jab. His eyes widened with surprise, and he exclaimed, "Man, that *is* solid!"

That wasn't good enough for my friend, though. "No! Really take a shot at it!" he exhorted.

Just as I turned and started to kindly advise my friend to shut his big fat mouth, the Bonecrusher let fly with a left hook that had every ounce of his nickname behind it. Lights flashed all around me as I bent over in agony. "Jesus Christ, Bonecrusher, what the hell is wrong with you?" I gasped.

Bonecrusher was full of apologies, and then slunk away to find someone else to torture, leaving me still trying to catch my breath. It felt as if my abdominal wall had caved in, and I actually had difficulty breathing for the next three months.

My whole weekend was ruined. Here I was on one of the proudest days of my life attending, in my honor, one of the great award ceremonies in boxing, and right on the dais I am nearly killed by a punch from one of its participants. All weekend the only thing I could think of was the famous magician Harry Houdini, who was also known for absorbing punches to his midsection. One day, caught unaware by a college athlete, Houdini was struck by a severe body blow that burst his appendix, causing peritonitis to set in. He died two weeks later.

As I lay in bed glumly recalling the ill-fated Houdini, I could only think of the worst. I could imagine the headline for that weekend: BOXER KILLS REFEREE WITH ONE PUNCH AT THE HALL OF FAME. I cringed at the irony. Despite Bonecrusher's boneheadedness, he hadn't meant to hurt me. I came away from the ordeal remembering to practice what I preach: "Protect yourself at all times!"

Baseball umpires aren't the only sports officials subjected to catcalls, curses and accusations of blindness by spectators who disagree with their judgment and handling of an event. Boxing referees, too, must endure fans' displeasure. It's unpleasant, but it comes with the territory, and you learn to accept it like a lab technician accepts hepatitis— as an occupational hazard. On one occasion, however, an unpopular decision almost cost me my life.

In 1966, I refereed a main-event bout between light heavyweight contenders Johnny Persol and Herschel Jacobs at the White Plains County Center in Westchester, New York. The arena was hot that night and the crowd even hotter. During the preliminaries, there were more fights in the stands than in the ring.

The Persol and Jacobs tilt was a ferociously competitive affair that had partisans on both sides screaming themselves hoarse. They were two evenly matched boxers, and after ten torrid rounds there wasn't much to choose between them. As I waited for the decision, you could feel the tension like an electric charge running through the arena. During these moments the crowd—like the unlit fuse of a powder keg—awaits the striking of a match.

The announcer collected the scorecards, and grabbing the microphone, he read the first one: "Judge Gamboli scores the fight five rounds for Persol, four rounds for Jacobs and one even." The second scorecard favored Jacobs six to four. That made mine the deciding vote.

The announcer paused for dramatic effect; the atmosphere crackled with anticipation. Then in a loud and unwavering voice he bellowed, "Referee Arthur Mercante scores the fight six rounds for Persol—"

That was as far as he got as the place erupted in a paroxysm of thunderous cheers ominously mixed with a cascade of angry boos.

After a controversial decision it's a good idea for the officials to head for their dressing rooms as quickly and inconspicuously as possible. Of course, that's often easier said than done, and in this case angry fans mobbed the ring apron and blocked the aisles, while local reporters peppered me with questions regarding the fight and the decision. It must have been a half-hour before I got back to the dressing room, but at least I arrived unscathed. I felt very hot and unusually tired. I sat down, closed my eyes and just absorbed the peace and quiet of my silent sanctuary. After a while, I even dozed off for a bit. When I awoke, I undressed to scrub off the sweat from my night's labors.

After a fight, some referees just jump into their clothes and head for home to take a shower. Not me. I can't bear getting into clean clothes when I am still hot and sweaty. Once under the shower, I began to feel better as the clean water cooled down my body. I stayed a long time, sudsing myself into a froth and luxuriating my tired and aching muscles until I was nice and relaxed. When I got out and dressed, I was surprised to see how late it was. I grabbed my bag and walked out into an eerily dark and silent arena.

All I could see was the illuminated "Exit" sign in the distance. Out of nowhere I remembered actor Robert Ryan, playing the boxer who'd refused to knuckle under the mob in the classic fight movie, *The Set Up*, finding himself afterwards all alone in a darkened arena haunted by the specter of unseen enemies.

Trying to keep my imagination in check, and with an uneasy feeling in the pit of my stomach, I walked toward the lighted exit, hearing nothing but the clicking sound of my footsteps. They seemed unusually loud. I was almost to the door, and starting to breathe easier, when suddenly a voice rang out in the darkness: "Hey ref!"

Startled, I turned toward the sound and, straining my eyes, I could make out in the dimly reflected light, the silhouette of a man moving toward me. "Yeah, ref, I'm talking to you," he said. I didn't know what he wanted, but I was pretty sure it wasn't my autograph.

"Hey man," said the voice, "where did you learn how to ref? Maybe I could go to ref school and learn to ref real good like you, huh?" I think the intended effect was sarcasm. He was now standing only a foot or so away, just glaring at me. I could make him out more clearly now. He was young and very angry.

"Well," I replied evenly, "I call a fight as I see it." Not a very novel riposte, but it got my point across.

"Just tell me one thing, ref," he said. "What fucking fight were you looking at? Because it wasn't the one I saw."

Then, with both hands, he shoved me backwards. That started my adrenaline flowing. "Now look, young man," I said forcefully. "I don't want any trouble with you."

"Well that's what you're going to get, ref—big fucking trouble," answered the punk, shoving me again.

Now I felt I had no choice but to put my bag down and defend myself. Though he was about half my age, I quickly sized him up and figured I could take him apart. What I didn't figure on were the four menacing figures that appeared out of the shadows as soon as I put my bag down.

My critic had brought a supporting cast, and with their unshaved faces and studded leather jackets, they looked like card-carrying members of the Hell's Angels. They all swore at me and made it clear that they had not come all the way down from Canada with Herschel Jacobs to watch their man get screwed by a guy in a bow tie.

Ref school hadn't prepared me for anything like this, and the notion of one guy dispatching five thugs only happens in Charles Bronson movies. I had to think fast or end up like poor Robert Ryan. So I switched gears and appealed for their sympathy. "Look fellows, you don't know how tough it was in there tonight. All right, so I blew it. I didn't mean anything against Herschel—he'll get another chance." I laid it on thick, telling them I was just a working stiff trying to support a wife and four growing boys.

My friend Anthony Quinn would've wept proud tears at such a dramatic snow job. Whether impressed or just stunned, my audience stood there like confused cattle long enough for me to grab my bag and head out the door. I made it to my car, and as I fumbled for my keys the herd came stampeding out after me.

"Let's get the son of a bitch!" one of them shouted.

Taking the cue, the son of a bitch leapt into his car and sped off. They were right behind me as we proceeded to drag race down the Bronx River Parkway. My gas pedal was almost down to the floor, but my pursuers accelerated even faster and, pulling even with me, tried to sideswipe me off the road. I swerved out of the way just in time. When they pulled alongside me a second time, I quickly slammed on my brakes. My car almost skidded out of control, but I managed to bring it to a stop, and as I hoped, the goons in the chase car went flying past me. Then, just like in some hot-wheeling Steve McQueen flick, I did a quick 180 and peeled off into oncoming traffic, no doubt causing blood pressures to spike stratospherically.

Somehow I didn't kill anybody or myself and got away from the Dukes of Hazzard with no worse than a near-case of cardiac arrest. When I phoned NYSAC Commissioner Edwin Dooley to report my close call, I heatedly told him how near he came to having one less referee in his employ. I told him it was appalling that the commission and the promoters did not provide boxing officials with security sufficient to keep them from the clutches of crazed patrons wearing studded leather jackets.

Edwin was very disturbed by the incident and said he would look into the matter. But he also admonished me. He told me that security precautions must begin with my own actions, that I had failed to exercise good judgment by isolating myself in a dressing room and not recognizing that there was safety in numbers, especially after a controversial decision.

There was a lot of horse sense in Dooley's remonstrance. I continued to take showers after a fight, but nothing of the grand opera variety—two minutes and I was out of there. It was no longer so important to get squeaky clean as it was to get home with no close shaves.

chapter 13

THE LIGHTER SIDE

R EFEREEING HAS its lighter side. In 1973, I was assigned to do the Jerry Quarry–Earnie Shavers fight at Madison Square Garden. This non-title fight created quite a stir since the talk was that the winner would get a title shot at the newly crowned heavyweight king, George Foreman. While only twenty-eight, Quarry had been a contender for years, having fought the very best, including Joe Frazier and Muhammad Ali. He and his trainer, Gil Clancy, were dying to get a shot at Foreman. Quarry had sparred with Foreman when Big George was climbing the ranks. Jerry told me that while Foreman was the strongest man he ever stepped into the ring with, he was convinced he could take him.

As many have noted, Quarry was a character right out of John Steinbeck's immortal novel, *The Grapes of Wrath*. One of those poor Okie types who had lived a hardscrabble life, this tough-fisted battler had become a compelling presence in the heavyweight ranks, not only because he was Irish and articulate but also because he was genuinely talented. But although fearless, hard-hitting and capable of counter-punching your head off, Quarry seemed to win every fight but the big ones. Now, after putting together a string of impressive victories, he was getting one last chance to earn a title shot.

Earnie Shavers was the same age as Quarry but not as well known nor seasoned. He had been around long enough, though, to be rec-ognized for his tremendous power. In fact, his last fight had been a one-punch knockout over former World Boxing Association Champ Jimmy Ellis, who defeated Quarry to win that title. Shavers's knockout percentage was simply incredible and many felt he hit even harder than the champion, George Foreman—a monstrous puncher in his own right.

Take it from one who has been watching fighters for seventy-five years: Shavers's punching power was no hype. He was one of the deadliest one-punch hitters I ever saw and several years later in a title bout, Shavers had Muhammad Ali out on his feet but didn't realize it and lost his chance and the decision.

Punching power is a heavyweight's greatest asset. Shavers and Bob Satterfield, a heavyweight contender in the early 1950s, were the two hardest punchers I ever saw who did not win the title—in fact, they were among the hardest punchers I ever saw, period. But they had something else in common, namely susceptibility to the other guy's punches or, in the parlance of boxing, a weak beard. Come to think of it, you can also throw Cleveland "Big Cat" Williams into the mix. When these bombers fought, it was as if decisions were outlawed. It was either they got you, or you got them—and most of the time they got *you.*

With all these ingredients brewing in the mix, Madison Square Garden was sold out for Quarry–Shavers. As I entered the ring that evening and began checking the ropes, I noticed ring announcer Johnny Addie about to make his way toward the ring to begin the introductions. Then from the corner of my eye, I spotted John Condon in the press row, mouthing something to me over the noisy buzz of the crowd. Straining to read his lips, I realized he was saying that the fly on my pants was open. But Condon, I knew, was a notorious practical joker, who liked to spring these little mind games on you right before a big event. Condon thought his pranks hilarious; I found them annoying.

So I ignored him, hoping he would get bored. But this only made Condon become more animated, and I began to feel a little self-conscious about having the president of Madison Square Garden Boxing pointing excitedly at my crotch in front of 15,000 people. I decided the matter bore further investigation.

I moved over to a corner cushion and, as quickly and discreetly as possible, brushed my hand over my pants and, to my horror, felt a gaping opening. Horror turned to full panic when I gingerly tried to zip up and discovered that the mechanism was broken. The main event would be starting in about ten minutes. I'm no exhibitionist so I had to do something fast or be humiliated not only in the Garden but also in front of a national closed-circuit TV audience. I must have startled more than a few fans and officials alike when I bolted from the ring and made a beeline for the dressing rooms.

There I ran into plain-speaking Teddy Brenner, the Garden match-maker, who was always on edge before a fight. "What the hell are you doing back here?" Brenner demanded. "The fight will be starting in a few minutes."

"Teddy," I said breathlessly, "do you have any safety pins?"

"What do I look like, Mercante, a fucking nurse?"

I explained what happened, and shaking his head in utter disbelief, he told me to go see Dr. Ziti in the medical office and have him sew me up. Dr. Ziti placed me on the rubdown table and performed flawless emergency surgery. He stitched me up nice and tight just in time for the main event in which Quarry got Shavers before Shavers got him. The fight lasted less than one round.

The early knockout had caused such excitement that when I got back to the dressing room I struggled to get my pants off before remembering that they were stitched up. I didn't want to rip them off because the pants were custom-made. So I re-entered the medical office and had the good Dr. Ziti undo his handiwork one stitch at a time. It was an especially intricate and delicate process because, in his haste to fix me up earlier, the doc had sewn the fly of my pants not only to my tee shirt underneath but also to my jock strap. A fraction deeper and I might have made history by becoming the first referee to be circumcised at a major sports event. Two weeks later, to my utter disbelief, I received a $25 bill from Dr. Ziti for services rendered. I sent the doc a personal check and chalked up another one to this loony business.

One evening I refereed a fight where one guy looked like Roberto Duran and the other guy had a look on his face like he was going to the electric chair. The fight started, and the Roberto Duran type was really out for blood. He'd come out of his corner, throwing haymakers but not really connecting. The other guy was white as a ghost, and when a glancing blow hit him, he collapsed as if he were an imploding building.

I started counting. "One . . . two . . . get up," I growled. "Three . . . four . . . get up, I said . . . five . . . six . . . I'm telling you for the last time, get up!"

The guy picked his face up off the canvas and with one eye open said, "Fuck you, you fight him."

In 1974, I was assigned to referee the Chuck Wepner–Randy Neumann fight in Madison Square Garden. Wepner was a big bear of a man whose ring career was distinguished more by gore and guts than boxing skills. Known as the "Bayonne Bleeder," Wepner had facial tissues that were so delicate it was said he began hemorrhaging during pre-fight instructions.

Because of Wepner's reputation for roughhousing and barroom brawling, I was concerned about the fight turning into a no-holds-barred street fight. When I walked into Wepner's dressing room to review the rules of the New York State Athletic Commission, I was especially clear that I wanted a clean fight and would tolerate no infractions. "Now Chuck," I said, "I want you to listen carefully: No hitting below the belt, no rabbit punching (behind the neck) and no punches to the kidneys."

Wepner's scarred features froze in mock horror, and he yelped: "Arthur, you can't do this to me! Those are my three best punches!"

Everyone there burst into laughter, including me.

True to form, the ring ran red that night, and most of the blood was Wepner's. A cut opened by Neumann was weeping pretty good, and I stopped the action to take a better look. As I appraised the damage, Wepner pleaded with me, "Please, Arthur, don't stop this fight—I signed to fight Ali, and I need the payday. Please, Arthur, please."

A referee must be deaf to emotional appeals, and I always tried to be. But while I didn't like what I saw, I decided to let the bout go on a little longer. Would I have stopped it if Wepner hadn't appealed so earnestly? Maybe. But fighting spirit counts—and Chuck had it in spades.

Fighting with a newborn desperation, Wepner turned the tide, and by the sixth round Neumann was actually bleeding worse than the Bayonne Bleeder himself and I could not let it go on any longer. I raised Chuck Wepner's big right arm in victory.

Chuck got his shot at Ali and fought the fight of his life. Though totally outmatched, outboxed and outgunned, Wepner won the hearts of the audience with his courage and determination in almost lasting the full fifteen rounds with the great champion. It was quite an emotional scene, with thousands of fans cheering for Chuck to go the distance, like something right out of one of the *Rocky* movies. In fact, it became the inspiration for the original *Rocky*.

One of the fans watching Ali–Wepner on the closed-circuit screen at a theatre was a struggling young actor. It was in the bedlam of that frenzied movie house, with the audience cheering Chuck on, that Sylvester Stallone dreamed up the idea of a movie about a broken-down, down-on-his-luck prizefighter getting the chance of a lifetime to fight for the richest prize in sports against a great charismatic champion. The story not only won the hearts of moviegoers but also the Academy Award for the best picture of the year.

Not long after *Rocky* won for best picture, Chuck Wepner stopped me at a boxing function. "You know, Arthur, I was the inspiration for the *Rocky* movie," he said. "But if you'd stopped that fight against Neumann, there would've been no *Rocky* movie and no Sylvester Stallone."

When I thought about that, I had to marvel at how a split-second decision could affect so many lives in so many ways. I was grateful that, in this instance, it was all for the better.

chapter 14

ROUND ONE TO THE LADIES

Boxing is rife with political and territorial jealousies, machinations, double-dealings and intrigues enough for a 007 movie. As I became more in demand as a referee, I would sometimes find myself embroiled in some dispute between commissions and their referees. There was then an unwritten rule in some states that required a referee to live in the state in order to be assigned to a match there. This proprietary arrangement angered some officials opposed to a closed shop but who weren't getting very far trying to change things.

So I was surprised when I received a call in 1971 from an official of the World Boxing Council who wanted me to go to Los Angeles to referee the Ken Buchanan–Ruben Navarro fight for the Lightweight Championship of the World. California was one of those closed-shop states, and refs who lived outside its borders weren't welcome between the ropes there.

When I wondered how my "Golden State" assignment was likely to be received, the answer was, "We don't care. This is a big fight and we want you to do it." But then came the political intrigue. He told me that I was to register at the Hotel Roosevelt in Los Angeles using the alias "Frank Robinson."

"Frank Robinson—like the baseball player?" I asked, somewhat bemused.

"Yeah, like the ballplayer—no one will confuse you for him," he said laughing. I wasn't amused, but when I said I didn't want to use an alias, he told me, "Look, Arthur, you know what a pain in the ass these guys can be. If you register under your real name, they will be on your scent like a pack of bloodhounds, and the whole thing could be derailed. Let's keep them in the dark till the last possible moment, so when they find out it will be too late to mount any opposition."

I reluctantly agreed, mostly because I believed it was wrong to keep referees from working in other states. I believed in a free market-place. Competition improves quality—and that includes the referee business.

I had just finished packing when I received a call from Bob Straile, who was the concessionaire for all the big sports franchises in New York. Bob and I had lunch the day before and discovered we both booked the same flight to Los Angeles. Straile was a big boxing fan. He was also debonair, immensely rich, a bon vivant and a renowned la-dies man, who would fill me in on his latest amours after we were done talking fights. Some of his conquests were high profile.

Bob was now calling to say that the press of business would keep him from going to California after all, and to ask for a favor.

"When you get to Los Angeles," Bob said, "call Zsa Zsa and tell her what happened." Bob was involved in a transcontinental romance with celebrity Zsa Zsa Gabor and never missed an opportunity to remind me of it.

"Gee, Bob, don't you think she would rather hear that from you than from a complete stranger?" I said, a little uneasily.

"I know, Art, but I promised her I would be there, and she doesn't take the word 'no' very easily, if you know what I mean," he said imploringly.

I didn't want to get involved and tried to opt out by reminding Bob that I had my hands full refereeing the big fight and weathering the political firestorm that would cause.

"Arthur," he pressed me, "Zsa Zsa is a very jealous woman, and if I call her she is going to accuse me of having another woman on the East

Coast and that is going to result in a bigger fight than the one you're refereeing. With business pressing so heavily on me today, I just don't need the aggravation."

Straile had done me some favors, so I couldn't refuse. I jotted down her number and promised to call. Before we hung up, Straile asked who I thought would win the fight. As a rule I never pick a winner lest people question my impartiality. But this time I thought an historical allusion wasn't out of line. "All I can say, Bob, is that Buchanan is a Scot, and history shows that the Scots have never been conquered."

I had a great deal of respect for Buchanan. He was not your stereotypical fighter, being very boyish looking, fair skinned and looking like he needed a good meal. Appearances can be deceiving though—especially in boxing.

Former Champ Lew Jenkins had arms like toothpicks, but he was the hardest punching lightweight I ever saw. Featherweight Sandy Saddler was another one who had to run around the shower to get wet; but he knocked out 103 guys!

Older guys told me about Panama Al Brown, who was nearly six feet tall but weighed only 116 pounds. They called him the "Human Xylophone," but when he whacked you the musical instrument you were most reminded of was a falling piano. Flyweight champ Jimmy Wilde looked like an undernourished child right out of the pages of a Charles Dickens novel, but they didn't call him the "Mighty Atom" because he was a firecracker. For his size (as tiny as 98 pounds), Wilde's punches were truly thermonuclear.

On the other hand, I've seen guys with muscles bulging like Popeye's after swallowing a can of spinach who couldn't knock a kid off a pair of roller skates. Boxing can be odd like that. I've seen guys who could take sledgehammer punches all night to the right side of the jaw without so much as blinking, but tap them on the left side and they're sleeping like a baby. Go figure.

Buchanan boxed stylishly to beat Navarro handily in fifteen rounds.

He was as impressive as he had been when he defeated Ismael Laguna, another talented boxer, to win the 135-pound championship. He looked like he would be on top for awhile. It was an easy fight to referee, and as it turned out there was very little grief about me getting the assignment. But I didn't stay long for interviews; no sense pressing your luck.

Up till then, everything had gone even better than expected. That ended when I picked up the phone and dialed the Hungarian sex starlet. Zsa Zsa delivered her signature greeting: "Hello, dahling!"

I started talking fast, "Miss Gabor, this is Arthur Mercante, and Bob Straile asked me to call to tell you he had to cancel his flight—"

"Who is this?" she interrupted. "Where's Bob?"

"This is Arthur Mercante, and I'm staying at the Hotel Roosevelt in downtown Los Angeles and Bob asked me to call you. I know that sounds strange, but this is not a prank. You could call me right back at the hotel if you like. This is the number, but don't ask for Arthur Mercante because I'm registered under the name Frank Robinson."

"What are you talking about? Who are you?" Before I could answer there was a click, and that was the end of my conversation with Zsa Zsa Gabor and of me running interference in Bob Straile's romances.

I did better with Miss America.

That she ended up in my home, exercising with me, I chalk up to one of those unpredictable but propitious happenings that we just stumble into by being in the right place at the right time.

In the early 1950s, I was a member of the Sun & Surf Beach Club in Atlantic Beach, Long Island. During the summer months I worked out regularly there, and my routine included some vigorous rope skipping. I was quite good at it, as good as most boxers, and my speed, timing and footwork would often attract a small crowd around me to watch.

The most famous member of the club, however, was Colleen Kay Hutchins, who was crowned "Miss America" in 1952. It wasn't hard to see why. Blessed with beautiful features and a classic hourglass figure, Colleen Hutchins didn't need to do any fancy rope skipping to attract attention. All she had to do was put on a bathing suit and casually stroll down the beach. Guys, including a fair number of geriatrics, would literally gawk at her. As a connoisseur of feminine beauty myself, I could not help but notice, although I sought to remain decently inconspicuous in my admiration.

Despite my acute awareness of her presence, as far as I could tell, Colleen Kay Hutchins was totally oblivious to my existence. In all the time I spent at the club, I never once talked to her. She broke hearts when we learned she had become a Mrs., marrying a Dr. Ernie Vandeweghe, who had played professional basketball with the New York Knicks before beginning a career in medicine.

So it came as quite a surprise when, on one terrifically stormy evening, our phone rang and on the other end of the line I heard a soft, almost purring, voice ask to speak to Arthur Mercante.

"This is he," I replied.

"Oh, hello Mr. Mercante. This is Colleen Hutchins, and my husband and I are members of the Sun & Surf Beach Club. We see you there quite often. My husband tells me you're a boxing referee, and you have been on television. I don't know anything about boxing but my husband is a fan and, well, I think it's very exciting—you being on TV and everything.

"I am wondering, Mr. Mercante, if I could ask you a big favor. You see, recently I received an offer to do a television commercial all the way out in Hawaii. Can you believe it? The part I'm playing calls for me to jump rope and—well—I haven't done that sort of thing since I was a schoolgirl. But I saw you do it at the club, and I could see you were just great at it. So I asked the manager who you were, and I took the liberty of looking you up in the phone book. You don't live far from us, and we're wondering if we could drive over and if it's not too much trouble maybe you can give me a few pointers?"

"You mean *tonight?*" I said, not quite believing what I was hearing.

"Why yes, I apologize that it is such short notice, but the scheduling of these assignments is beyond my control. I have no choice but to be there this weekend or I lose the assignment. So, as you can see, time is of the essence, and it is such a great opportunity for me that I want to be as prepared as I can."

"Gee, Mrs. Vandeweghe—"

"Call me Colleen," she purred.

"Ahem, yes—Colleen—I would love to help out, but this is the worst possible night. My wife and I have been up with our baby boy for the last two evenings. He's a colic baby, you know, and with all this thunder and lightning, tonight he is worse than ever."

"Colic baby, huh? Well you know, Mr. Mercante—"

"Call me Arthur," I purred.

"Yes—Arthur—my husband is a pediatrician, and you know he is just so wonderful with babies and little children. If you want, he could examine him and see if there is anything wrong and maybe even get him to go to sleep. In the meantime you could, you know, show me your technique. How does that sound?"

Frankly, with Gloria and me being at our wits' end trying to stop the baby's crying, the idea sounded great. But then again—who am I trying to kid?—wits' end or not, I was tickled pink over the idea.

Within a half-hour they were at our front door. While Dr. Vandeweghe went upstairs with Gloria to attend to the baby, I took Miss America downstairs to our homemade gymnasium. Up close she looked even lovelier, and I was quite taken by her natural beauty. As an athlete she wasn't bad either, and before too long Colleen could skip to a number of different routines.

By the time we said good-bye to the Vandeweghes, Colleen felt confident about mastering her new assignment, my son was sound asleep, and even the heavy thunder and lightning had finally stopped.

As I stepped outside to walk them to their car, my beaming, ear-to-ear smile would've put Bert Parks to shame.

Then there was the time in 1967 that I boarded a flight to Mexico City where I was scheduled to referee a fight. I was just about to settle down when I noticed other passengers hurriedly leaving their seats and gathering to the rear of the first-class section.

Curious about all the activity, I inquired what all the commotion was about. The flight attendant told me that movie star Raquel Welch was on the plane and was signing autographs. Her most recent film, *One Hundred Rifles,* co-starred Burt Reynolds and football great Jim Brown. The interracial love scenes with Brown, controversial for the time, raised quite a few eyebrows among both film critics and movie audiences.

Gazing back to the rear of the plane, I could see Raquel, wearing a clinging mini-skirt with a form-fitting blouse that unabashedly advertised her movie star assets, to say the least. Believe me, everything about her exuded a raw and unbridled sexuality.

When we landed in Mexico City I immediately exited the plane so I could get a better look at Raquel when she deplaned. As I stood waiting for her, a man approached and asked, "Are you Arthur Mercante?" When I replied affirmatively, he identified himself as a television reporter there to cover my arrival for the eleven o'clock news. Boxing was—and still is—a hugely popular sport in Mexico, and even lowly referees were accorded celebrity status.

The reporter told me I had come off the plane so fast, they were unable to capture my arrival on film. I was instructed to go back up the stairway into the plane and then re-emerge waving my arms and smiling. I did as I was told and thereby cast poor Raquel into an unaccustomed supporting role. All of a sudden the other passengers deserted her to take a gander at this mystery man all of Mexico was waiting to see. Was he a movie star? A famous entertainer, maybe? A big shot politician? My fifteen minutes of fame in Mexico came to a screeching halt when my identity became known, whereupon the audience dispersed amidst general grumbling about phony celebrities.

Raquel was a good sport about being briefly upstaged. She approached me and with a ravishing wink said, "I never knew that a boxing referee could be such a sex symbol."

I hadn't been knocked so dizzy since Ernie Terrell clocked me on the chin.

chapter 15

THE KING & I

I N MY TRAVELS I have logged over a million miles of flight time and have not only been to nearly every state in the Union but have refereed fights all over Europe and Asia, and have traveled to Moscow and Australia.

Traveling is one of the great bonuses of this job, and visiting so many different countries has enlarged my perspective. It has given me both a cosmopolitan outlook and a deeper appreciation of the blessings of being a citizen of the United States of America. It has been said many times, but still not often enough, that we who live in America are the most fortunate people in the world.

Not that my travels around the globe have been unpleasant; indeed, the very opposite is true. Not only have I received enormous pleasure enjoying and learning from the many different cultures and peoples I have come in contact with, but I have always been treated with the utmost respect and graciousness.

One of my most memorable experiences abroad came when I traveled to Thailand in March 1970 to referee the Efrén "Alacrán" Torres–Chartchai Chionoi fight for the WBC Flyweight Championship of the World. Upon landing I was cordially greeted by a polite young man wearing a yellow Hawaiian shirt who ushered me into a limousine that hurried me off to my hotel in Bangkok.

There everyone seemed to be terribly interested in my comfort and well-being. In fact, I began to feel a little embarrassed by all the attention that was showered upon me every place I went. Even in my dressing room at the arena there was a bottle of champagne on ice for me. As I said—things couldn't be nicer.

Just before the introduction of the fighters, the arena grew dark and a spotlight was focused on a huge procession marching toward ringside. Some eight sturdy looking men were carrying a beautifully adorned, gold-laced carriage, on top of which sat an older man covered with a long flowing robe. I didn't know what was going on and wondered if the Pope himself had purchased a ticket for the fight.

The men carefully placed the throne at ringside where I got a better look and was relieved to see it was not the Holy Father after all. Noticing my puzzlement, one of the officials whispered in my ear that the personage before me was no less than the King of Thailand, who was renowned for, among other things, being a rabid fight fan.

I had seen movie stars, big-wheel politicians and all manner of other celebrities in attendance at championship fights, but never a king, throne and all, sitting at ringside. The whole atmosphere seemed utterly surreal, and every time I looked over at His Highness, I half expected to see Yul Brenner from *The King and I*.

The fight was waged at a terrific pace between two determined, courageous little battlers. When it's flyweights in there, you are with fighters who can move; and you have to be ready to move with them. I had a lot of experience with these two fighters, having refereed their two previous encounters in Mexico City, both of which had plenty of high-speed action. This third go-around, however, was the best of them all, and after fifteen rounds of hard fighting, Chionoi was awarded a unanimous decision.

As I exited the ring, the spectators were still wildly cheering both fighters. Before I got to my dressing room, I was told that the King wished to grant the two fighters and me a royal audience. Of course I replied that I would be honored, and with the two fighters I was escorted to His Majesty's throne.

Having never met a king before, I naturally felt a bit unsure over propriety, or even how I would communicate with him, since we spoke different languages. But the potentate put the three of us instantly at ease by placing garlands around our necks and addressing each fighter in his native language. This command performance had hardly registered when the King turned to me and said in flawless English (I would later learn that he was a Harvard graduate), "And you, sir, are a great referee. My compliments, Mr. Mercante."

Flattered by the Royal compliment, all I could think to do was to bow awkwardly and say, "Thank you very much, Your Majesty"—it wasn't much of a salutation but, hey, it was an improvement over Jim Thorpe's laconic, "Thanks, King" when the Royal Sovereign of Sweden called him "The greatest athlete in the world."

Not long after I was escorted back to my hotel room, there was a knock on my door. I answered and a young officer with an army sergeant greeted me. I recognized him as the man in the Hawaiian shirt who had met me at the airport earlier that day. Smiling widely, he explained that he was the King's nephew, and he was under Royal orders to show me the very best of Thai hospitality.

That night another luxurious limousine ferried me to all the sights and delights of this exotic country. I was served lavish and sumptuous meals, the finest wines and desserts. I began to feel a little like royalty myself and a little guilty that Gloria was back home missing all the fun.

As this wonderful evening wound down, I was taken to the King's palace itself. The grand splendor and utter magnificence of His Majesty's residence was literally breathtaking. Elegance was everywhere. Even in those wee hours, servants were busily preparing the next day's meals. In a kitchen of mammoth proportions, I was struck by the variety of foods prepared and arranged in the shape of exotic fish or flowers or some other object. But the most delicious dishes were still to come.

Invited to peer through an enormous mirror, I saw dozens of the most beautiful young women, lasciviously lounging in a next-door room. While I could see them, it was explained, they could not see me. It took a few moments for it to dawn on me that what I was looking at was the King's very own harem. His Majesty had come a long way from Harvard Yard!

Moving about in the bejeweled scene of championship boxing, I was no stranger to beautiful women. But nothing could have prepared me for this or what was to come. Amid this glowing galaxy of female pulchritude, I was invited to choose the woman that most pleased me. I explained, as tactfully as I knew how, that while I greatly admired and appreciated the beauty before me, I was happily married and not in the market for female companionship. They seemed astonished (even though married themselves) at my declination. I was a little astonished myself, but to my great relief they were not insulted and respected my wishes.

By that time I was exhausted, and my hosts took me back to my hotel where I slept soundly. After all, a great championship fight, an Epicurean banquet, the company of a king and a harem housing the most exquisite feminine creatures imaginable—how much excitement could a man stand in one night?

chapter 16

SMOKIN' JOE

I N THE LATE 1960s, the heavyweight division was in the throes of a schismatic struggle to find a successor to Muhammad Ali. The heavyweight champion had been defrocked for his refusal to be inducted into the army. Ali's declaration that he had "no quarrel with them Viet Cong" resulted in his exile, and he was no longer allowed to earn a living by fighting.

New York and four other states decided to anoint the winner of a fight between Joe Frazier and Buster Mathis as the new Heavyweight Champion of the World. But not so fast, said the rest of the world. Who made New York the final authority? Well, New York did. Long known as the Mecca of boxing, "the city that never sleeps" asserted its prerogative with typical chutzpah and declared the winner of the match would be the world champion—period!

The World Boxing Association—which had been feuding with the New York State Athletic Commission since the early 1930s, when it was the National Boxing Association—protested angrily. What about all the other worthy contenders, not to mention the other states and countries represented by the WBA?

In response, the WBA organized what it called a "Fair Elimination Tournament," involving contenders Floyd Patterson, Ernie Terrell, Thad Spencer, Leotis Martin, Jerry Quarry, Jimmy Ellis, Oscar Bonavena and Germany's Karl Mildenberger.

As a referee, I stayed outside the political bickering, kept my opinion to myself and awaited assignments. The New York State Athletic Commission selected me to referee its world championship fight between Frazier and Mathis.

For some time I had been watching the progress of both fighters. They had met in the amateurs, with Mathis beating Frazier to become the United States representative to the 1964 Olympic Games in Tokyo. But when Mathis injured his hand in training, Frazier suddenly found himself on the U.S. team and wound up with a gold medal.

"Olympic gold," however, did not immediately open the door to riches and glory. Maybe it was because Frazier was Mathis's replacement and therefore considered illegitimate by the fans and boxing elite alike. Or perhaps it was because Frazier did not physically match some people's ideal image of a heavyweight fighter. A graceless, squat stump of a man, Frazier relied on hyperaggressiveness, unusual stamina and a big left hook to overcome his opponents. For whatever reason few promoters beat a path to Frazier's door.

Boxing writer Bob Thornton, my dear friend and one of the keenest observers of the sport, was convinced from the very start that "Smokin' Joe," as he was called, had the grit, iron and power to be champion. It still had to be proved to me, and now I would have a chance to see him up close and personal.

Frazier–Mathis was one of the two championship fights to inaugurate the new Madison Square Garden on March 4, 1968. The other more legitimate title match was between Nino Benvenuti and Emile Griffith for the middleweight championship. It felt a little odd having Griffith on the card and not being the referee, I had officiated so many of his bouts. The important thing, however, was that I landed the headliner, the one deciding Ali's replacement—at least for five states.

When I got to the Garden that night the air was thick with tension. But it was not just the usual fight night anticipation. The deposed champion, Muhammad Ali, had become a political lightning rod. The Black Muslims, the black separatist outfit with which Ali was aligned, announced that its members were not going to let white people dictate who the heavyweight champion was when everyone knew it was Ali. Parading around the Garden was an army of Ali supporters with huge signs condemning what they called a championship charade. Pictures of the former champion were everywhere.

Inside the new Garden, though, things looked pretty much like the old Garden: the same red velvet roped ring and the organ music; the same announcer, Johnny Addie; the same cigar smoke, billowing up in funnels and floating about like cloud formations.

The usual retinue of former champions and colorful contenders were introduced. For a bit of Garden nostalgia, old-time Light Heavyweight Champion Paul Berlenbach made a grand entrance. His fight with Jack Delaney opened the old Garden on Fiftieth Street and Eighth Avenue back in 1925. Contrary to some recent ugly rumors about my age, I did not referee that fight.

I chatted with former heavyweight contender Tony Galento. Tony briefly had Joe Louis on the deck in their 1939 title fight and was one of the strangest looking characters who ever stepped in the ring. Both shorter and wider than Joe Frazier, Galento stood maybe five foot eight inches tall; but he seemed five foot eight whichever way you looked at him.

Called "Two Ton Tony" and "The Beer Barrel That Walks," Galento trained on cigars and beer and would do crazy publicity stunts like sparring with bears and kangaroos. The circus atmosphere got plenty of press and laughs; in the ring, however, his opponents were hardly amused by this wild, swinging, carnival caricature. Galento could knock you stiffer than the proverbial two-by-four. Like Frazier, The Beer Barrel had two qualities that elicited respect from the boxing fraternity: an almost unbelievable physical toughness and a left hook that could take your head off. It's a lot harder to get power behind your punches when you reach up. But this never occurred to Galento, who specialized in cutting guys down—like Buddy Baer, Max's outsized brother, who stood nearly a foot taller than Two Ton. When a reporter asked, "Tony, how do you explain your ability to punch up?" Galento, the squinty-eyed pugilistic philosopher, huffed, "Punch up, punch down, what the hell's the difference?"

When the Frazier–Mathis go started, it looked like boxing had another talented curiosity in the 243½-pound Buster. I was amazed how someone his size could be so light on his feet. I had him winning five of the first six rounds. But Frazier, though outweighed by some forty pounds, never stopped coming. Though he was behind and sometimes even made to look foolish, Smokin' Joe Frazier smoked. Like "The Little Engine That Could," nothing human was going to stop his train of destiny.

Frazier's body punches echoed loudly throughout the new Garden. His left hook dug holes in Mathis's enormous bulk. Slowly the bounce disappeared from Buster's legs, and Frazier, breathing hard but snorting fire, planted his head on Mathis's chest and chopped down Mount Mathis much like those sides of beef he used to butcher in the Philadelphia slaughterhouses.

The eleventh round spent Mathis. A couple of thunderous body shots followed by a left hook to the head and Buster flopped backward through the ropes and landed halfway on the outside of the ring apron with a seismographic thud that must have registered on the Richter scale. His chest was splattered with blood, and his huge torso heaved with exhaustion. Buster struggled up at the count of eight. I looked at his bloody face and vacant eyes and stopped the fight.

Frazier was now champ—or was he? "Not according to the WBA," and even louder were the cries of protest from Ali's supporters. Loudest, as usual, was Ali himself. Cannily turning it into a racial issue, he called Frazier "the white man's champion" and an "Uncle Tom," doing the bidding of the political and racial establishment whose roots were deep in the slave–master culture of the nineteenth century.

It was an ugly tactic, the worst kind of psychological warfare. But it had the desired effect among many young Americans who came to believe Frazier was a traitor to his race. Frazier, a proud man, who was twice as black as Ali, and who grew up twice as poor, seethed with resentment.

Joe and his manager, Yank Durham, a wily old fox, retaliated by always referring to the former champion not by his adopted Muslim name but, instead, by what Ali considered his slave name: Cassius Clay. The last guy to show such temerity toward the champion was Ernie Terrell, and he suffered the consequences of being humiliated and tortured by Ali throughout their fifteen-round affair.

I am often asked if the animosity between Ali and Frazier was an act to build the gate. Believe me, this was no hype! Their mutual malevolence fueled the egos of both, a volatile mix in this high-stakes game for sport's most prestigious prize. Together, they were like nitroglycerin.

In the ring, Frazier was proving himself to be a fighting champion. I know because I refereed several of those championship bouts. He destroyed Manuel Ramos (the tallest Mexican I ever saw) in a furious firestorm of punching. He took on Dave "The Animal" Zyglewicz, whom he blitzed in less than a round, and in a classic slugfest he out-punched and brutalized tough Jerry Quarry to the point where I refused to allow Quarry to come out for the seventh round. Everyone agreed that Frazier was the roughest, toughest, gutsiest fistfighter to come along since Rocky Marciano ruled the roost. For all that, many felt Frazier was the best heavyweight in the world only as long as Ali was busy sparring with Uncle Sam. For a proud man like Frazier, hearing this caveat grated on him like fingernails on a blackboard.

All this was part of the mosaic of the vast social upheaval of the

1960s: civil rights activism, political assassinations and the polarization of the Vietnam War resulted in riots in every major American city. Each fighter became a symbol for some larger political cause. Just as President Kennedy felt compelled to tell then Heavyweight Champion Floyd Patterson that for the image of the Negro race it was imperative that he defeat Sonny Liston, now I heard that President Richard Nixon was openly rooting for Joe Frazier to zip the Louisville Lip—permanently!

History is a distant mirror, and I could see the reflection of the 1960s in the decade of the 1930s when Heavyweight Champ Joe Louis met Germany's Max Schmeling in a clash freighted with political symbolism. But then Americans were united against Schmeling, who was made to represent all the evils of the Aryan race, Hitler and Nazism. President Franklin Roosevelt actually met Joe at the White House, felt the champion's muscles and proclaimed them the kind of muscles we were going to need to defeat Nazi Germany. Louis wiped Schmeling out in the first round in what was considered a great victory for all of America and the free world. But the '60s were different. With the advent of sex, drugs and rock & roll, Americans were polarized, frequently along cultural, racial and generational lines. It wasn't a pretty picture.

While Frazier ran up more successful title defenses, Ali, the deposed champion, constantly fanned the political fire building under the two of them. When Joe defended against Oscar Bonavena in Philadelphia, Ali, sitting at ringside, received a bigger ovation than did Frazier, the hometown champion. To throw salt in the wound, Ali dismissed the bout as a match between two sluggers, no championship fight. After Frazier earned general overall recognition as champion by KO'ing Jimmy Ellis, who'd won the World Boxing Association laurels, Ali demeaned the victory by saying that Frazier had done nothing more than beat up his former sparring partner.

In 1970, Ali regained his license to box and started on the road to Frazier at a sprint. Within just six weeks, Ali defeated top contenders Jerry Quarry and Oscar Bonavena. The Bonavena conquest was especially delicious for Ali and his supporters, since Ali became the first man to ever stop the Argentinean strongman. Bonavena had not only gone the distance twice against Frazier but also in their first fight bounced him off the canvas twice.

The momentum was now rising to flood tide. It was a match that Ali, Frazier and the public demanded. I was anxious for it myself, though of course I didn't have any idea then that in the coming fistic storm, I would be in the eye of the hurricane.

chapter 17

THE MANASSA MAULER

T HE NEW Madison Square Garden wasn't all blood and gore for me. Boxing had its lighter moments. In 1970, it became the venue to celebrate Jack Dempsey's seventy-fifth birthday. Everyone in the Garden stood up and sang "Happy Birthday" to the great "Manassa Mauler." Dempsey had fought once in the Garden—the old, old Garden that is, back when it was actually located in Madison Square. That was when he knocked out Big Bill Brennan in the twelfth round back in 1920. The knockout came none too soon: for the last two rounds Dempsey's ear was hanging by a thread.

Even at seventy-five, Dempsey was still a powerfully built man and had the rough-and-ready look of a real fighter. I got to know The Mauler well when shooting the movie *Requiem for a Heavyweight*. As I stood off to the side waiting for my cue for the next scene, Jack's wife, seeing me all spiffed up and spanky clean, asked if I was "a Hollywood referee or a real referee."

"No, Mrs. Dempsey," I assured her, "I'm the genuine article."

"Well, you look so right for the part, you could be from Hollywood," she chirped.

As the champ looked on, amused, I thanked her for the compliment.

On the outside, Jack Dempsey appeared the perfect gentleman, the classic restaurateur and boxing's goodwill ambassador. But underneath the polished veneer one could sense danger lurking, a man who, once aroused, was still capable of pitiless violence. In his fighting prime, Dempsey was known as the "Man Killer," a giant slayer who changed boxing from the clutch-and-hit style typical of those scheduled forty-five-round affairs to a blitzkrieg attack designed for total destruction in the shortest time possible. His almost maniacal go-for-broke, bob-and-weave style electrified fight fans all over the world and ushered in the first million-dollar gates in ring history. Jack Dempsey made boxing an indelible part of the emerging American sports culture after the First World War.

The first fight I can personally recall is the second Dempsey–Tunney fight, the famed "Battle of the Long Count" in 1927, which I listened to on our gramophone radio back in Brockton, Massachusetts. I was only seven years old, but I remember the excitement as if it were yesterday. That's how it was with Dempsey. He lost that fight after having Tunney on the canvas for what seemed an eternity; but the Manassa Mauler would remain, next to Babe Ruth, the biggest name in sports in the first half of the twentieth century.

There was an aura that surrounded Dempsey. Even my hard-to-impress uncles were in awe of him. Everyone was. He was like a "big cat," Uncle Joe would tell me; on his feet "the most dangerous man in the world," Uncle Neib would quickly add. As a young, upcoming fighter himself, Uncle Joe watched Dempsey train. He told me how, after a fight or a rigorous workout in the hot sun, Dempsey would sit in the shade and slake his roaring thirst with an ice-cold beer. I made it a habit to do the same, first as a Golden Gloves boxer and then as a referee. If it was good enough for the great Dempsey, it was good enough for me.

During the filming of *Requiem for a Heavyweight*, Dempsey regaled me with stories about his hardscrabble youth when he was coming up in the ranks. Perhaps no champion ever had to overcome such adversity. One of eleven children in a poverty-stricken home, Dempsey

began street fighting at age seven. At sixteen he was on his own, sur-
viving on the money he earned digging coal and whatever he made
with his fists. He would fight anywhere: the saloons, the docks, deep
in the mines or just for survival in the hobo jungles he frequented.
These pick-up fights were often life-and-death struggles with no padded gloves or bells to signal rest periods.

"I was only a kid and some of those big miners would outweigh me
by almost 100 pounds, but I murdered almost all of them," he told me
as he gritted his teeth and clenched those big maulers of his.

Jack described how he filled a flower sack with sand, hung it from a
rafter in an old barn and hammered away at it until his knuckles were
so raw he couldn't stand to hit the bag anymore. He bathed his face
in sticky beef brine to toughen his skin against cuts and chewed raw
gum that oozed from scrub pine trees to strengthen his jaw. He built
a 3½-foot cage and for hours on end would practice his crouching
bob-and-weave style inside it. Dempsey traveled from fight to fight by
holding on for dear life to the beams underneath railroad freight cars.
One slip meant certain death.

I was riveted by Jack's stories: how he became champion by mas-
sacring giant Jess Willard under a broiling sun in Toledo, Ohio; how
he fought Georges Carpentier at Boyle's Thirty Acres, boxing's first
million-dollar gate; how he stood up to 3½ incredible minutes with
Luis Firpo, the "Wild Bull of the Pampas." In ringdom's most savage
fistfight, Dempsey had to literally climb back into the ring to knock
out the Argentinean mastodon after he was sent sprawling outside the
ropes.

Famed boxing trainer Ray Arcel told me how Dempsey's colorful
manager, Jack Kearns, ruined Dempsey by keeping him inactive during most of his championship years. A fighter with Dempsey's hell-for-
leather style needed action, Arcel told me, and plenty of it. Instead,
Kearns had Dempsey making those crazy movies in Hollywood. It was

driving Jack crazy. Meanwhile, none of the deserving black contenders of that era ever got a shot at his title, even though Dempsey had fought some black fighters before he had been champion.

Ever since the highly controversial Jack Johnson (who, by the way, also drew the color line by not defending his title against black contenders), black heavyweights had gotten a raw deal, and the word was that Dempsey was afraid of Harry Wills, the top black heavyweight of the early '20s. Nonsense, said Uncle Joe. Ridiculous, said Ray Arcel. Dempsey's top sparring partners were black, including George Godfrey, who was even bigger than Wills and almost as good. The way Dempsey would manhandle Godfrey left no doubt among these observers that he would have dispatched Wills if they had ever met.

"Wills was big, and none too fast," Arcel told me. "It was a terrible injustice that Wills never got a title shot—colored fighters always got the short end of the stick, but those big, slower guys were made to order for Dempsey."

My most cherished personal memory of Jack Dempsey happened years before *Requiem*. It was New Year's Eve 1942, and I was dating a girl in the service named Nonny Horton. Nonny piloted the planes ferrying supplies and men across the Atlantic. These women fliers were the great unsung heroes of our war effort, and the important role they played still has not been fully addressed by World War II historians.

Nonny and I decided to celebrate by having dinner at Jack Dempsey's Northwestern Hotel on Fifty-seventh Street in Manhattan. Jack was a U.S. Coast Guardsman himself during the war and loved military people. Seeing us sit at a table, he came over to say hello. He couldn't have been nicer. I mentioned that I was doing some refereeing in the service, and you'd have thought from his effusive reaction I was officiating championship bouts at the Garden. The old champ knew how to make a twenty-two-year-old guy look like a million bucks in front of his date.

Later, Jack sent to our table an expensive bottle of champagne on the house. As we looked over at his table, Dempsey lifted his glass and toasted us. He was a champion in a lot of ways.

I came along a little too late for Jack Dempsey to be the idol of my boyhood. Dempsey belonged to my uncles' generation, and when they would gather around and talk, it seemed as if there could be no other heavyweight champion than the great Dempsey. No matter who was champion of the moment, the title would always belong to him. Sitting there on that New Year's Eve of so long ago, and watching the Manassa Mauler toast my date and me, I felt the magic, and at least for a night, I knew how they felt.

chapter 18
THE FIGHT OF THE CENTURY:
Ali–Frazier I

MARCH 8, 1971

Just seconds before the bell for the first round, I glanced over at Muhammad Ali's corner, watching him assume his customary prayerful pose before the start of his first fight with Joe Frazier. Ali had been quoted as saying he wanted fifteen referees at this fight "because there ain't no one referee who can keep up with the pace I am going to set." I aimed to prove that just one referee would be ample. In a way, I had been in training my whole life for this night myself.

Having refereed quite a few of Frazier's fights, I knew that despite his aggressive, ferocious style, he was basically a clean fighter. Ali was mostly a clean fighter, too, but he did do a few things on the inside that were illegal, such as grabbing a fighter behind the neck and pushing his head down. Because he was Ali, some referees looked the other way; but I was determined to enforce the rules regardless of who I was in the ring with.

The bell rang and Ali circled quickly to his left. Predictably, Frazier came right at him in that bob-and-weave style of his. It was all fight and fury right from the start. They didn't call him "Smokin' Joe Frazier" for nothing.

When one is in the middle of officiating a great sporting contest, the very drama and immediacy of the event make it difficult to later recapture your thoughts as they occurred at that very moment. But even now, more than thirty years later, several things stand out very clearly in my mind.

In the early rounds Ali was very sharp, very fast. In fact, he was hitting as crisply and as hard as he ever hit: one-two punch combinations that were right on target. They were mean, vicious combinations, enough to discourage any fighter in the world from moving in on him—any fighter that is, except the one coming out of the opposite corner.

Frazier came at Ali incessantly, but every time he would land his vaunted left hook, Ali would shake his head derisively to assure the world that Joe could not hurt him. The first two rounds were clearly Ali's, but Frazier was setting an ungodly pace and that left hook was getting dangerously close to the mark. At the bell ending the third round, Frazier landed a sizzling left that jarred Ali. It was the best punch of the fight thus far. I noticed that as Ali walked to his corner he wasn't shaking his head anymore, though he himself was clearly shaken.

In the early rounds, both fighters surprised each other. Frazier's nearly super-human persistence and his ability to get inside of Ali's long arms must have been disconcerting to the former champion; while Ali's ability to withstand Frazier's heavy artillery must have been no less surprising to the champion. Remember, at this time Ali's extraordinary capacity to take a punch was not widely heralded, or even realized, for that matter.

Throughout the fight, Ali kept up a constant chatter. I admonished him several times to stop the talking. He would stop for a while and then begin baiting Frazier all over again. He was trying to psyche Frazier out, but it clearly wasn't working. By the seventh and eighth rounds, Ali just laid against the ropes, throwing pitty-patty punches in rapid succession as Frazier hammered furiously at Ali's body. I thought Ali better get off those ropes because he was going to end up giving away valuable rounds. Then again, he had to be tired from the unforgiving pace Frazier had set and, knowing that his legs could no longer carry him a full fifteen rounds, he was probably trying to conserve energy.

After losing the first half of the ninth round, Ali suddenly awakened with a series of blinding combinations that rocked Frazier down to his heels and, at least momentarily, slowed Joe's forward momentum. Ali had gotten his second wind, and he looked magnificent, rattling off a series of punches that made it the best round of the fight for him.

In the tenth, I experienced one of the most embarrassing moments of my entire career. Frazier was a bull of a man, and with his high-speed, fast-forward style I sometimes had to use physical force on him to get him to back up from a clinch. Whenever I ordered them to break, Ali would just float back while Joe, like a runaway locomotive, kept right on chugging forward. This happened about midway through round ten, and as I charged in to assert my authority the little finger of my extended right hand jabbed Frazier sharply in the bottom of his eye socket.

Incensed, Frazier turned to me and growled, "Goddammit, man, keep your fucking hands off of me." Then, turning to his corner, he complained bitterly to Yank Durham, "Damn it, Yank, I've got two fuckin' guys banging on me now!"

Right then a terrifying thought flashed through my mind: What if Frazier decided on the spot that he wasn't going to fight anymore, with both Ali and Mercante taking pokes at him? The "Fight of the Century" would, thanks to me, become the controversy of the century.

Thank God it didn't happen. When I put my arm around Joe and gently pushed him back into action, he and Ali went at it hot and heavy until the bell sounded.

Usually the only time I ever visited a corner after a round was when I believed a fighter to be hurt or when I needed to warn him about some persistent infraction of the rules. But I felt awful about what happened, so during the one-minute rest period, I went to Frazier's corner to apologize, and Yank, who labored in the railroad yards for years, was not a man to mince words. Durham reamed me out in a language that was just a tad stronger than the Queen's English.

After ten rounds of non-stop fighting, I had Muhammad Ali ahead. But although Frazier's face was turning into a mass of lumps and bruises, from the eleventh round on it was mostly Joe's fight. He staggered Ali badly in the eleventh, and Ali was hurt more than at any time since the first Hank Cooper fight when the left-hooking Englishman had Ali down on the deck. He began to mock Frazier, exaggerating how hurt he was by swaying all over the ring, but it could not camouflage the fact that he had been rocked, and rocked badly.

The twelfth and thirteenth rounds were not as punishing for Ali, but still it was Frazier's sheer, unrelenting aggressiveness that was making a bigger impression than Ali's pretty combinations. The pace of the fight continued to be astonishing. In the fourteenth round, Ali somehow managed to get back up on his toes and actually won the round handily. It was Ali's last hurrah. The table was set for a dramatic climax.

It's the last round of this epic battle that most people remember best of all. Me, too. I couldn't believe that these two warriors were leaving their stools to answer the bell for the fifteenth round. They had thrown some of the best punches I ever saw, and here they were, after forty-two minutes of toe-to-toe fighting, still ready to go at it. It was boxing at its best.

Just twenty-five seconds had elapsed from the sound of the bell when Frazier, wild eyed with determination, reached back and landed a tremendous left hook to Ali's jaw that sent Ali crashing to the canvas. It was an incredible moment. Ali had not hit the boards in eight years, and the sight of him down there was shocking. Cameras recording the historic moment flashed all over the Garden like some crazed laser show while fans shrieked both in horror and delight at this unexpected scene.

I motioned Frazier to a neutral corner, and Joe went right there.

When I turned back to Ali, I was astonished to see he was already up. The right side of his face was swelling badly, making him look like he had a bad case of the mumps. But he was clear-eyed and in control of his faculties. I never once thought of stopping the fight. In fact, Ali was competitive for the balance of the round, and by the time the bell sounded Frazier was the more exhausted of the two. In the last thirty seconds they clinched, and I had to be very careful separating them for fear that one or the other might fall over if I pushed them apart too hard.

These two athletes had given everything they had for the right to be called champion. No matter who won or lost, both qualified for the designation. For all its ballyhoo, no fight ever more justified its buildup than Ali–Frazier I.

One judge, Arthur Aidala, scored the fight nine rounds to six for Frazier; another, Judge Bill Recht, somehow scored it for him eleven rounds to four. My scorecard read eight rounds for Frazier, six rounds to Ali and one even. The fight was close, sure, but there is no doubt that Frazier won even if Ali managed to convince legions of his supporters that he was the true victor that night, a claim he would later recant. If the fight had been scored on the points system—the most equitable way to score a fight—Frazier's margin of victory would have been greater, for he would have won not only the fifteenth round by two points but, in all likelihood, the eleventh round.

But the closeness of the fight had more to do with the tremendous toll the match took on both fighters. Frazier had to be hospitalized, and although only twenty-seven years old, his best days as a fighter were behind him. Though some of Ali's greatest victories still lay ahead, he would never again approach what he once had in his prime, as he did that night.

New York City has been called the city that never sleeps. It was never more so that night. Celebrations and talk of the fight echoed throughout Manhattan. Two spectators in the Garden had actually suffered fatal heart attacks from the excitement. On his way back from the fight, Jack Dempsey, seventy-six years old, knocked out two muggers outside his restaurant on Broadway. Clenching his big-knuckled right fist he told me later: "I can't go long, Arthur, but I can still punch a little."

As for the referee of that historic fight, once the decision was announced I called it an evening. I went straight home to be with Gloria and the boys. The next morning, at nine o'clock sharp, I was back at my desk at Schaefer Breweries, ready to start another day's work.

chapter 19

THE GREATEST

I T WOULD BE impossible for me to give a complete accounting of my seven decades as a boxing referee without talking about the colossal figure of Muhammad Ali. It has always been a point of enormous professional pride that I refereed some of his most significant championship matches.

Whenever a giant walks on the world stage it is always difficult to assess, without prejudice or partiality, his true impact on the times in which he has lived and the legacy he will leave. So I will leave that large and important task to the historians and pundits, and just share with the reader some personal remembrances and observations that I have made about his extraordinary life and career.

The only place to start when discussing Muhammad Ali is with what first made him famous: his boxing skills. They were supreme.

His most conspicuous attribute was his blend of size and speed. When he was young he could move with a swiftness and athletic grace that has never been matched. Although never a great knockout puncher, Ali's offense was mind-boggling nevertheless. Possessing a beautiful left jab, Ali's blinding combinations had a devastating cumulative effect on his opponents.

He had his critics, of course. They said his constant motion was extravagantly wasteful, that he kept his hands too low, that he pulled away from punches instead of slipping them. Ali was guilty of all these things, but because of his unique physical gifts this unorthodox and even reckless style was perfectly suited to him.

While his ability was recognized early on, few thought he had a chance against the awesomely powerful and supposedly unbeatable Sonny Liston. The "Big Ugly Bear," the sobriquet with which Ali mocked Liston, was considered to be the most menacing man on the planet. I saw brave fighters—big, strong heavyweights—literally freeze at the mere sight of Liston.

I met Sonny several times. At six foot one inch, he was by no means unusually tall for a heavyweight, but he was a giant locked in a six-foot-one-inch frame. Specially tailored collars and pants had to be made to fit his huge neck and thighs; his fists resembled boulders, the biggest of any heavyweight champion (including the six-foot-six-inch, 270-pound Primo Carnera); and his wingspan stretched an incredible eighty-four inches. But his most menacing feature was that cold stare. Liston's eyes were like bottomless pits; they seemed lifeless when they looked. It was an eerie feeling. Floyd Patterson was totally unnerved by Liston's evil eye, and was KO'd by Sonny twice in the first round.

None of this seemed to strike terror into the heart of young Cassius, who would stick his tongue out at Liston, and ridicule and taunt him at every opportunity. Even those who wore a badge or carried a gun did not treat the "Big Bear" with such disrespect. In fact, many sportswriters thought Cassius was either whistling in the dark or was certifiably nuts.

Their February 25, 1964, title bout was a revelation. The twenty-two-year-old Clay gave a masterful boxing performance, cutting Liston up and making him quit in his corner. It was a shocking upset. Equally shocking was Clay's announcement that he had become a Black Muslim and was changing his name to Muhammad Ali.

As if controversy and his athletic ability were not enough to attract attention, Ali had a natural charm which, combined with his extraordinarily good looks, made him an irresistible force in life and especially to the mass media, which sought his attention as much as he sought fame and recognition.

It was love at first sight between the press and Ali, who possessed an unparalleled genius for self-promotion. He elevated bragging to an art form: even before he won the title, Ali unabashedly called himself "The Greatest," tagged his opponents with ludicrous nicknames and composed juvenile doggerel, predicting with almost unerring accuracy in what round his opponent would fall. This gift for prophecy amused and delighted his many fans as much as it annoyed and angered his legion of detractors. It all added up to tremendous business at the box office.

When he returned to the ring after his 3½-year exile caused by his refusal to enter the army during the Vietnam War, Ali's skills, while still remarkable, were diminished to the point where he could no longer move three minutes a round, and his reflexes were just a heartbeat slower. Moreover, a tougher crop of heavyweights had emerged than those he faced during his first championship reign.

The period of 1970–1976 was the golden era of heavyweight boxing. Along with Ali, there were Joe Frazier, George Foreman, Ken Norton, Jerry Quarry, Jimmy Ellis, Oscar Bonavena, Earnie Shavers and Ron Lyle. Yet even the Ali of diminished skills was victorious ten out of twelve times against these formidable opponents.

His two greatest victories were the fight against George Foreman (a young reincarnation of Sonny Liston) to win back the championship ten years after he beat Liston, and his third fight with his archnemesis, Joe Frazier. (The rubber match with Frazier, the "Thrilla in Manila," was one of the most brutal and glorious fights ever waged for the heavyweight championship.) In those two fights, as well as in his first fight against Frazier, Ali revealed another quality that would prove both a blessing and a curse: a frightening ability to absorb blows to both the head and body.

This remarkable resilience took an awful toll, and the truth is that after his third fight with Joe, Ali was fighting on borrowed time. All that remained of his extraordinary skill was his ability to absorb punishment and his mastery at clinching, the excessiveness of which was technically illegal and outrageously ignored by some referees in Ali's later fights. Ultimately, that was not enough, and at the end of his career he suffered humiliating defeats at the hands of Larry Holmes and Trevor Berbick that rank among the saddest fights in boxing history.

Over the years, however, the legend of Ali has grown even larger. This is because Ali has been so much more than just a prizefighter, more than even a champion. He was a man of his times.

Muhammad Ali's long battle with Parkinson's disease has made this mythical figure more like the rest of us, a human being struggling with the pain and limitations of his humanity. Indeed, Ali has taken the final leap in the American consciousness, transcending sports, politics and partisanship to become not only a folk hero but a national heirloom, not only one of the most famous figures in the world but one of the most cherished.

A few years ago I was invited to the opening of a new gymnasium in New York City. The special guest was to be Muhammad Ali, and on a whim I thought I would bring him a gift. Stopping at Bloomingdale's, I bought a large box of Godiva Chocolates. I told the girl at the counter who they were for and, genuinely affected, she tenderly wrapped the chocolates in beautiful gift-wrap paper.

When I arrived at the gymnasium, there was a long line of fans, waiting to get autographs from Ali. Spotting his daughter Laila (the spitting image of her father and now a successful boxer herself), I told her I was unable to stay and wondered if she would give him this box of candy for me.

Her eyes lit up. "Oh, candy! My father loves sweets!"

I told her it was Godiva Chocolates.

"Chocolates!" she said excitedly. "They're my father's favorites—how did you know?" Grabbing my arm, she led me to the front of the autograph line. "Look, Daddy, Arthur Mercante brought you a box of Godiva Chocolates."

Ali got up, hugged me affectionately and whispered almost inaudibly in my ear: "My ref." I was deeply touched. His hands were shaking badly, and he looked tired and feeble, but as he embraced me I could still feel his strength. He took the box of chocolates and began unwrapping it gingerly, tenderly, as if it were a diaper on a newborn baby.

His daughters gathered around him and before long the box was empty. Apparently, the whole family shares Ali's weakness for chocolates. I never even got to taste one. It didn't matter. I was happy and content just to bask in the magic warmth of his glow. It is like that every time I am with Ali. It's a special feeling, something that never grows stale but is always new. It is the kind of feeling that takes you back to your childhood again. Even at my advanced age, I still get that same thrill whenever I am with him. I suppose it will always be that way, no matter how old he gets, or how old I get—for I am, and always will be, Muhammad Ali's biggest fan.

chapter 20
RIVALS OF YESTERYEAR:
Joe Louis and Max Schmeling

I N 1973, I was invited to the Coliseum in Nassau County to honor the achievements of amateur boxing in the United States. To bally-hoo the event, the sponsors invited former Heavyweight Champions Joe Louis and Max Schmeling in commemoration of the thirty-fifth anniversary of their legendary second fight. The sponsors flew Schmeling all the way from Germany, where he was a millionaire businessman. It had been years since he had been back in the United States.

The sight of the two great champions and former rivals meeting and then embracing each other was electric. Their 1938 title match was so rife with political and racial symbolism that it remains one of the most pivotal sporting events of the twentieth century. I was just eighteen then, but even the passing of more than sixty-seven years has not dimmed the memory of the excitement, anticipation and controversy that swirled around that fight.

Although I was a big Joe Louis fan, I felt a pang of sympathy for Schmeling's predicament. When you think of it, it is hard to see how any fighter could have fought in a worse climate than Schmeling did, meeting Louis for the title right here in New York City.

In June 1938, Hitler's policies of massive rearmament and territorial expansion, and his persecution of Jews made Nazi Germany the enemy of the civilized world. Schmeling, just by virtue of his nationality, became an extension of that. His oft-stated disclaimer, "I am an athlete not a politician" and the fact that he had a Jewish manager, Joe Jacobs, did not cut any mustard with Americans, who mocked him at public appearances by goose-stepping with their right arms aloft—the signature salute of the Third Reich. Yet through it all, Schmeling conducted himself with an innate grace and dignity that I always admired and respected.

I also felt for Schmeling because we had a family connection of sorts. My uncle Joe Monte had fought Schmeling in Max's American debut back on November 23, 1928. Uncle Joe told me that Schmeling was the best man he ever fought and by far the hardest hitter. Nevertheless, my uncle put up quite a battle until Max lowered the boom in the eighth round with a paralyzing right hand to the body that left Uncle Joe prostrate on the canvas. Decades later my uncle would still wince describing the knockout blow.

With the possible exception of Gene Tunney, I believe Schmeling was the best heavyweight in the years between Jack Dempsey and Joe Louis. Superbly conditioned, possessing a rock-solid chin and a deadly right hand, Schmeling was a brilliant strategist, who had a genius for discovering and exploiting an opponent's weakness. This was never more in evidence than in his first fight with Joe Louis in 1936, when Max capitalized on Louis's penchant for dropping his left hand after throwing a jab, and knocked Joe out in the twelfth in one of boxing's greatest upsets.

"Hello, Max," I said at the Coliseum. "I'm a nephew of Joe Monte; you fought him back in 1928. It was your first fight here in America. I don't know if you remember my uncle, but he sure remembers you. He tells me you nearly killed him with that right cross of yours."

"Remember him? Yes," said Schmeling in his heavy German accent, his thick black eyebrows arching up in surprise. "He was a real tough fighter. Tell me, is he still living?"

"He sure is," I replied, "back in Brockton, Massachusetts, and he would love to talk to you." Schmeling was staying at the Waldorf-Astoria Hotel. He gave me the phone number and told me to have Uncle Joe call him early the next morning.

They spent a half-hour reminiscing about the old days. It was a record for my uncle, whose phone conversations usually consisted of "hello" and "good-bye." I felt a great deal of satisfaction in bringing my uncle and Schmeling together and seeing once again the special fraternity boxers share with one another, a fraternity born of the pain, struggle and loneliness that fighters uniquely experience.

As much as I admire Schmeling, for me, as for so many others, no one stood on a higher pedestal than his rival, the great "Brown Bomber," Joe Louis. I suppose it is impossible to be entirely free of one's generational prejudices, but I truly believe that at the height of his physical powers he was the greatest heavyweight I ever saw.

Joe Louis was simply boxing history's most potent combination puncher. He threw bombs in blinding succession from either side, his punches usually traveling no more than six inches. There might have been two, possibly three, heavyweights who hit harder with one punch than Louis—but combination for combination, no one else matched Louis's punching skills, which represent, for me, the very height of athletic prowess.

To those who believe Muhammad Ali was the best heavyweight ever, you go right on believing that. I'm not trying to persuade anyone; but don't try to convince me to change my mind, either. I saw both fighters up close and personal when both were in their physical primes. Ali was a ring marvel and, in my opinion, among the heavyweight champions he comes the closest to Louis in pugilistic greatness.

Newspaper columnist Jimmy Cannon put it best after Joe destroyed Schmeling just two minutes and four seconds into their second fight: "Joe Louis is the greatest fighter I ever saw or expect to see. One day someone will beat him. But no one will ever beat the Joe Louis you saw last night." Amen.

But Louis was more than just a boxer; his contributions transcended sports. He did more than any other athlete to win acceptance for African Americans in both sports and society. Ignorance caused some to accuse him of kowtowing to white society, but the truth is that it was Joe's quiet strength and sincere patriotism that built the bridge Jackie Robinson would cross almost ten years later to change American sports forever, and for the better.

When some reporters baited him for going into the army while black people were still segregated, not only at home but in the armed forces themselves, Louis, the semiliterate son of an Alabama sharecropper, rendered them mute by simply stating, "Whatever is wrong with America, it ain't nothing Hitler can fix." There was so much truth and dignity in Joe's one-liners, and America loved him for it.

The last time I was in Washington D.C., I visited Arlington Cemetery and the headstone marked with the name of Joseph Louis Barrow. His last years were painful ones marked by bankruptcy and mental illness. In that beautiful, quiet setting, I stood silently before his grave, awed by the distance of years when, as a youngster, I stood not in respectful silence but lustily cheered his name. Gazing at the monument, I uttered a quiet prayer of gratitude, knowing the great champion is at rest where he rightfully belongs, among our honored dead, forever a part of our national memory.

chapter 21

WHAT'S MY LINE?

T HANKS TO REFEREEING, I've had the opportunity to do TV com-
mercials and appear on numerous television shows. I appeared
with the brilliant comedian Ernie Kovacs on his show *Take a Good
Look,* and I was also on the popular quiz shows *What's My Line?* and *To
Tell the Truth.* In 1974, I made a guest appearance with Joe Frazier and
Muhammad Ali on the kid's show *Wonderama* with two of my sons.

After consulting with me, the producers decided because of the bad
blood between the two fighters, they each would appear separately
with boys I brought from the Echo Park boxing program. Frazier came
on first and demonstrated how to hit the heavy bag.

Next came Ali, who, as always, stole the show. He play-sparred with
the boys and in typical Ali fashion, declared himself vastly superior to
the Echo Park boxers when he was their age. But when Ali saw a boy
skipping rope like a pro, he was impressed. The show's host told him
that was Tom Mercante, son of the man who refereed Ali's first fight
with Frazier, who happened to be sitting in the audience.

I was called up on stage, and with a theatrical glare Ali said, "I don't
know if I should shake Arthur's hand, since he robbed me when he
voted for Joe Frazier when I really won."

I just smiled. But my boy Tom (God bless him) took umbrage at the
insult directed at his old man and in an attempt to save family honor,
told me that I should whip Ali right then and there. It was just the
opening Ali was looking for.

"So you think your daddy could whup me?" he asked Tom, his eyes popping in astonishment at the boldness of my youngster.

"That's right," said Tom, motioning for me to teach Ali a lesson.

I guess I could have thanked my son for the vote of confidence, but instead I gulped and began to understand why lions eat their young. But nobody enjoyed the scene more than Ali, who then warmly shook my hand. By the time we left, Ali's antics had us all in stitches. It was great entertainment, and the boys and I loved appearing with these two great champions.

My appearance on *To Tell the Truth* came after the first Ali–Frazier fight. Part of the CBS prime-time lineup, *To Tell the Truth* featured four celebrity panelists whose job was to ask questions of the three contestants all claiming to be the same person and, from their answers and demeanor, determine who was telling the truth. The show began with a brief recitation of my boxing resume, emphasizing the recent "Fight of the Century." Then the curtain went up, revealing two others and me, and one-by-one we each stepped forward claiming to be Arthur Mercante. The two imposters were my brothers, Al and Ralph. We all looked enough alike, although both of my brothers topped six feet, while I'm around five foot seven inches tall.

I had prepped my brothers on everything I could think of about boxing to make them credible imposters, and they were doing great. I wasn't so bad myself. When a panelist—the always-likable Gene Rayburn—asked me what division Nijinsky fought in, I told him Nijinsky was a ballet dancer not a boxer. Gene gave one of those big, devilish smiles of his and said, "Oh well, I thought I would try to get a sneak punch in there."

With three panelists down and one to go, it looked like the Mercante brothers would make a clean sweep of things. The panel looked completely baffled. All except for the last member, that is, and before you knew it actress Peggy Cass had Ralph and Al on the ropes. Turning to

Al, she said, "Contestant Number Three: What division did Fritzie Zivic fight in?"

Right away a big red flag went up in my head. I thought, Fritzie Zivic has not been in the sports pages for thirty years. How in the world does she know about Fritzie Zivic? If I was surprised by the question, you could imagine how poor Al felt.

"Well," Al said, "I think Zivic fought as a middleweight."

Ooh, I thought, Al blew it; Zivic was one of the roughest, if not *the* roughest, welterweight champion ever. He busted up Henry Armstrong something horrible in one of their fights and knew more dirty tricks using his thumbs and laces than anyone in memory—and was damn proud of it. They said the worst insult you could pay Fritzie Zivic was to tell him that Harry Greb fought even dirtier.

You could tell right away that Cass knew Al was whistling Dixie. Like a skilled prosecutor, she *sensed* weakness and probed deeper.

"What city did Fritzie Zivic fight out of?" she asked next. Anyone involved in boxing as long as I knew Zivic and Pittsburgh were as inseparably linked as Boston and Red Sox baseball slugger Ted Williams.

"Uh," said Al, starting to squirm just a bit in his seat, "it was Chicago."

With a look of pure triumph, Peggy now turned the heat on Brother Ralph: "Contestant Number One: How many Zivic brothers were boxers?"

"Um, I think he was the only one," Ralph said hesitantly. With that answer, I knew my brother Ralph, the podiatrist, had put his foot in his mouth. They were known as "The Fighting Zivics," and there were five of them.

If I had been scoring, the Mercante Brothers would have taken the first three rounds. But that last round was all Peggy Cass—at least a 10–7 round, with her scoring a couple of clean knockdowns.

When it came time to vote, the other three panelists went with

Ralph or Al, but Peggy Cass correctly fingered me as the real Arthur Mercante based on my brothers' deficient Zivic awareness. I told her that if she ever got tired of the acting business, she ought to go to work for *The Ring* magazine.

When Ralph and Al introduced themselves as my brothers, the audience applauded, and everyone got a real kick out of it. But no one enjoyed the show or each other as much as we did. My fellow contestants could've used a little brushing up on their boxing history, but life couldn't have blessed me with two finer brothers.

I also had a lot of fun doing commercials. I did an Oldsmobile commercial, another one had me selling Zenith television sets, and for another product I even played a referee. It wasn't typecasting, though, because instead of officiating a boxing contest, I reffed a wrestling match. When the hero put the villain on his back, I pounded the canvas three times for the pin.

My most memorable commercial, however, was not for television but rather radio. I received a call from the backers of a product called "Sock It," a cleansing agent for backyard pools. They told me that former Middleweight Champion Rocky Graziano would be on the commercial, too, and would I like to be part of it also? Would I ever! I loved Rocky—everybody did.

The rags-to-riches story of Rocky Graziano was well known. He was the tough-as-nails juvenile delinquent, who became notorious for stealing and fighting in the streets. Rocky hung around with another street tough, who served time, became middleweight champ and had a movie made about his life—a guy named Jake LaMotta. "Me and Jake really weren't so bad," Rocky told everyone. "We only stole things that began with the letter 'A'—A wallet . . . A radio . . . A car . . ."

After several stints in reform school, Graziano joined the U.S. Army and was later imprisoned and dishonorably discharged for punching out a superior officer. Rocky, for sure, had trouble with the law, but he also had two things going for him—a winning personality and a right hand that, when it landed, had the same effect as swallowing a whole bottle of sleeping pills. Paul Newman played Graziano in the superb movie adaptation of Rocky's autobiography *Somebody Up There Likes Me*. Rocky always joked that Newman won the part because "he looked like me before I started fighting."

Since we were about the same age, I had my own youthful memories of Rocky Graziano, and they were thrilling. In the immediate postwar years, Rocky was the hottest property in boxing, outstripping, for a time, even Joe Louis. He exploded on the scene in 1945 with a sensational third-round knockout of young Billy Arnold. That name doesn't mean a thing today, but back then Arnold was considered a boxing prodigy with championship potential.

Rocky just destroyed Arnold, who was so traumatized by the savage beating he was never again the same fighter. It wasn't just the knockouts that electrified fans, it was the way Rocky went about butchering his foes. Teeth bared, swinging for blood with every blow, Rocky fought with a blind rage that bordered on the homicidal. It was more of the same when he demolished Marty Servo and Freddie "Red" Cochrane, both of whom were welterweight champions at the time they fought Graziano.

Then came his breathtaking trilogy of fights with Middleweight Champion Tony Zale, still regarded as the most brutal in the 160-pound class. Rocky won the title in the middle fight, sandwiched between two KO's by boxing's "Man of Steel."

After his three wars with Zale, the fire in Rocky had burned down to an ember. Sugar Ray Robinson knocked Graziano out, and then Rocky lost to welterweight Chuck Davey, a former college champion. After hanging them up, Rocky struck it rich in, of all things, show business. His charisma, his gregariousness, his god-awful diction landed him a regular role on Martha Raye's TV program. The more Graziano mispronounced words and mangled his lines, the more audiences loved him. He ended up a fixture on the talk show circuit and a ubiquitous commercial pitchman.

We met for the commercial at a Manhattan studio, and Rocky ran right over and gave me a bear hug. But the director, a bearded, serious-looking man was all business and nothing for conversation and good company. "Let's get rolling," he ordered.

We were briefed and handed a small script to study. My part was that of a ring announcer introducing the former Middleweight Champion of the World for an important announcement about Sock It, a new formula guaranteed to knock out all the germs and bacteria in your pool thanks to something called "super-chlorination"—whatever the hell that was. It was obviously important, though, from the way the director kept telling Rocky to stress it for all he was worth.

So we began. I introduced Rocky, who wasn't doing too badly until he had to say "super-chlorination." His face contorted as he wrestled with his tongue, only to blurt out not super-chlorination but "super-formation."

"Cut! Cut!" the director yelled. "No, no, Rocky, not super-formation, *super-chlorination!*"

Another take, another introduction of Rocky by me, another pitch by the champ of Sock It. Rocky went on telling the world that Sock It would KO bacteria because of "super-urination."

The words "Cut! Cut!" reverberated off the walls. "*Super-urination!* Rocky, what the hell are you trying to do, kill the product?" blurted our bearded Cecil B. DeMille.

In between takes I took Rocky aside and gave him a short lesson in pronunciation. It must have looked pretty comical: the two of us, standing face-to-face in the corner mouthing the syllables "su-per-chlor-in-a-tion." Rocky pronounced it slowly . . . very slowly.

"I think you got it, Rock," I exclaimed.

"I think so too, Art," he said, grinning happily.

Everyone seemed amused by our little exchange except the director, who sat there, drumming his fingers and rolling his eyes. "If you are finished with your English lesson, Mr. Mercante," he said icily, "we would like to finish up before we break for supper."

It came out "super-cremation" on Rocky's third try, and young Cecil B. went off the deep end in a super-chlorinated frenzy. One more mistake, he said to Rocky, talking like a schoolteacher to a recalcitrant student, and he was out on his ass. To do that to anybody was rude; to do it to Rocky Graziano was rude and incredibly stupid. The Rock took a step toward the guy and his intention obviously wasn't to discuss directorial technique.

"Wait, Rocky," I said, stepping in harm's way. Rocky had knocked out fifty-two opponents in his career, and the director, who turned pale, was about to become victim number fifty-three. "This isn't worth getting yourself in trouble," I said, trying to cool him off.

"Yeah, yeah, you're right, Art," he said, calming down a bit. Then turning back to the director, Rocky said, "Just answer one question, ya little punk." With four fingers he jabbed at the little DeMille's shoulder: "How much money did ya make last year?"

"What does that have to do with making this commercial?" the director asked meekly.

"Answer the question, how much ya make?"

"Eighty-eight thousand," the director stammered.

"Eighty-eight thousand! Eighty-eight thousand!" Rocky said incredulously. "Ya wanna know what the Rock made last year—ya wanna know? The Rock made two hundred ninety-two thousand! And ya wanna know somethin' else, smart mouth? If I talked good like you, ya bum, I would have made what you made."

Rocky broke everyone up with that line, and even little DeMille let out a silly grin. After that, with just one or two minor mishaps, the commercial was wrapped. And it wasn't even noon yet. Rocky felt like celebrating with a drink and invited me to join him at Toots Shor's place. When I pointed out that Shor's wasn't open for business so early, Graziano told me not to worry: "They'll open up for the Rock."

Well, it's nice not to worry and, after all, how do you say no to Rocky Graziano? On our way, I turned to the champ and said, "You know, Rocky, every day you learn something new. Even this morning I learned something."

"Like, what?" Rocky said.

"Well, I never knew how many words in the English language rhymed with 'chlorination.'" We both enjoyed a hearty laugh over that.

It was a beautiful morning in Manhattan, and everybody was out and about. Everyone seemed to know Rocky: the cops, the hardhats, the cab drivers, the doormen and even the pretty young girls. The streets were full of salutations: sounds of "Hiya, Rocky," "Hey, Champ," "Keep punchin', Rock," filled the city air. The people loved it, Rocky loved it, and I loved it.

"Rock," I told him, "when I come back in another life I want to be you."

Rocky knocked on the locked door of Toots Shor's located just off of Sixth Avenue.

A gruff voice on the other side said, "We're not open."

"Hey, it's me: Rocky; let me in."

"Sorry, Rock," the man said, "I didn't know it was you."

Sitting at the bar I ordered a club soda. It wasn't even lunchtime, for God's sake.

"How 'bout you, champ?" said the bartender to Rocky.

"Give me a snifter of Courvoisier," the Rock said, pronouncing each syllable with distinct perfection.

I almost fell off my stool. He hadn't taken as much punishment from Tony Zale as he did trying to say "super-chlorination" all morning; and here was "Cour-vois-i-er" tripping off his tongue like he was William F. Buckley Jr. himself! "Rock, I can't believe it."

"Believe what, Art?"

"How could you pronounce a difficult French word so beautifully and have so much trouble with 'super-chlorination'?" I asked.

Savoring his first sip, Rocky smacked his lips and said, "'Cause, 'super-chlorination,' Art, ain't brandy." Then the former Middleweight Champion of the World toasted me and downed the glass of Courvoisier with one mighty and triumphant gulp.

chapter 22

MAYHEM IN JAMAICA

T HERE WERE PREMONITIONS. You could feel them, even if you could not place your finger on anything out of the ordinary. At least this was the mood at the Sheraton Hotel in Kingston, Jamaica, where I was staying and where Heavyweight King Joe Frazier was preparing for his 1973 title defense against George Foreman.

I should not give the impression that there was a sense of impending doom surrounding Frazier. There wasn't, not by a long shot. The general feeling was that the fight would be a good one while it lasted, and in the end Joe Frazier would have his way with the heavily muscled 1968 U.S. former Olympic champion.

There were, however, a few dissenters here and there. The loudest of them was Howard Cosell, his ungainly physique looking ridiculous as he paraded about the hotel in his Bermuda shorts. He was telling everyone within earshot that the world was going to be shocked, shocked (sounding like Claude Rains in *Casablanca*), when Foreman KO'd Frazier in two rounds.

It didn't seem likely, yet ever since I arrived in Kingston on January 19 the Frazier camp looked like anything but the headquarters of a fighter getting ready to defend the most prized title in sports. The atmosphere just wasn't right; it was too relaxed, too festive. There were parties, barbecuing and songfests long into the night. Frazier seemed to be more focused on his second career as a rock singer than on preparing for a heavyweight title fight.

There were other troubling indications, such as Frazier's inactivity. In the nearly two years since he defeated Ali, Joe had defended his title only twice, both times against journeymen opponents, who actually rocked the champion before Frazier dispatched them. Clearly, Frazier had not been showing the same fire and firepower that had pulverized Jimmy Ellis and Bob Foster, and had sent Muhammad Ali crashing to the canvas.

As for George Foreman, I never saw a hair of him until the weigh-in on the morning of the fight. He looked honed and massive, much bigger than the 217½ pounds registered on the scale. The talk was that he had been training in secret up in the mountains. The few reporters who had access to Foreman's camp told stories about the huge amounts of tape he used on his hands to protect them from the seismic impact of his blows on the heavy bag. They brought back spine-tingling accounts about how Foreman committed mayhem on the bag, hammering cavernous holes in it and hitting it almost as if it were a speed bag.

It all sounded ominous, but for all we knew, it was just the usual overblown hype ladled out to impressionable reporters by publicists since John L. Sullivan wore the crown. Foreman was still very much an untested quantity who was undeniably powerful but also ponderous; whereas Frazier, after all, was the conqueror of the great Ali.

Having previously been third man in the ring for both fighters gave me insights on their fighting qualities. Frazier, I knew, was a great fighter, usually superbly conditioned and incredibly aggressive. While he was not a two-handed puncher, he had one of the fiercest left hooks I ever saw. But just like most other knowledgeable observers, I was also less than impressed by his most recent performances and physical condition.

As for big George Foreman, I had refereed two of his fights. I knew he was immensely strong and a very powerful puncher, indeed. I also knew that he was faster than a lot of people thought. His problem was that he threw his punches in wide arcs, often telegraphing their arrival and leaving himself wide open for counters. That could be fatal against a left-hooker like Frazier who could get in and punch inside those big swinging arcs and hammer home his heavy artillery.

The fight was to be held at Kingston National Stadium, an arena built to host track meets, not boxing matches. Before the fight, I made a mental note to myself to watch for the rough stuff. Foreman was not above using it, and I wanted to get it in hand before it got out of hand.

Dick Sadler was training Foreman. His cousin was the early 1950s featherweight titlist Sandy Saddler, a mean, vicious puncher, who wouldn't know the Marquess of Queensberry from Marilyn Monroe. Though a great fighter, Saddler just savaged the rulebook. I saw his roughhouse, free-for-all style overcome Willie Pep's boxing brilliance three out of four times in their classic series.

I also remembered Foreman's fight with Boone Kirkman, which I refereed. At the opening bell, Foreman charged across the ring and actually bulldozed Kirkman to the canvas as if he were Dick Butkus tackling some hapless quarterback. I bawled him out good and threatened to disqualify him if he tried anything like that again. I had no trouble with George after that, but Kirkman did, even though the youngster from Seattle had one of the savviest boxing men around in his corner, "Deacon" Jack Hurley. Nearly twenty years earlier, Hurley had brought another tiger from the Pacific Northwest to town and touted him as a surefire champion. But Rocky Marciano plastered Harry "Kid" Matthews in the second round, and Boone Kirkman fared no better against Foreman, whose sledgehammer blows practically decapitated Hurley's champion.

At the center of the ring, Frazier and Foreman greeted each other with long icy glares freighted with menace. The bell sounded, and I could feel the bounce of the canvas and the cool Jamaican night air brushing lightly against my cheek as I moved into position.

It was over in 4½ electrifying minutes. The dethroning of a champion and crowning of a new heavyweight champion is undoubtedly one of the most thrilling events in all of sports. What occurred in those few minutes, on the night of January 22, 1973, was all of that and much more. No one in that open-air arena was prepared for the dramatic, explosive and shocking scene that would unfold before their disbelieving eyes.

It was Joe Frazier who got in the first good blow at a rather tense-looking challenger. But then Foreman began to loosen up, keeping Frazier from crowding him with monstrous left jabs that had "Sonny Liston" written all over them. Suddenly, Frazier was down. He rose quickly, appearing unhurt as I tolled off the mandatory eight-count. Having come so unexpectedly, the first knockdown stunned the over-flowing crowd into silence; but as Foreman continued his assault the arena erupted into total bedlam.

Foreman's blows were no longer wide or ponderous but delivered rapidly with a compact and concise deadliness. Foreman's pile-driver punches drove Frazier to the ropes, the last place in the world the champion wanted to be. Incredibly, Foreman was manhandling one of the most ferocious heavyweights in history as if Joe was a mere schoolboy. Raining blow upon blow, each one a haymaker, Foreman again capsized Frazier with a tremendous uppercut. Frazier was hurt and dazed but got up quickly and amazingly revived his senses as I tolled the mandatory eight-count. I actually had to restrain Frazier from getting back at Foreman too quickly. This guy was one tough son of a bitch.

But Frazier wasn't upright long. A series of one-two power punches sent him sprawling to the canvas just before the bell rang. Since the rules called for the count to continue after the bell, I kept counting. In other words—there would be no saving by the bell. Mightily, Frazier struggled to his feet and staggered back to his corner, where his handlers frantically administered smelling salts.

The minute's rest wasn't enough for Joe. He started round two pitching leather, but a short Foreman right staggered him. The crowd noise was deafening, but I could still pick out Angelo Dundee's high pitched, panicky voice piercing the Caribbean night air: "C'mon, Joe, baby, hang in there! C'mon, Joe, baby!" Muhammad Ali, desperate for a rematch with Frazier, had sent Angelo to Kingston with the instructions "make sure nothing happens to Joe Frazier." But things were happening to Joe Frazier, all of them bad.

Foreman began to violently shove Frazier to the ropes. It was exactly what I was on the alert for. I jumped between them and issued a strong warning to Foreman, prompting George's apoplectic handlers to jump on the ring apron screaming, "Let them fight! Let them fight!" Of course I ignored them; no one was going to tell me how to do my job. As it turned out, my intervention offered only a momentary respite for Frazier, who was undergoing the worst aerial bombardment since *Thirty Seconds Over Tokyo*. Joe was bludgeoned to the canvas for a fourth and then a fifth time.

Tradition calls for giving the champion every chance, a point I honor but never at the expense of the fighter's personal safety. Even after the fifth knockdown Frazier was still lucid, still ready to fight, still throwing punches back, or at least trying to. At moments like this, every referee walks a tightrope. In a split second a referee must rely on his own best judgment. I decided to let it continue, although I felt Frazier's fate was sealed.

Foreman ended it with a huge half-right uppercut. It was not a snapping, concussive punch, but the sheer force of it lifted Frazier nearly six inches off the ground—a frightening testament to Foreman's Herculean strength—and deposited him on the canvas in a messy heap. Frazier, being Frazier, got up, but now blood gushed from his mouth and he stumbled about the ring. I waved my arms and embraced him, signaling an end to the carnage and the crowning of a new heavyweight champion.

It was, by any measure, an incredible performance by the new champion. Along with Joe Louis punching Max Schmeling into a quivering wreck, it was, cumulatively speaking, the most overpowering demonstration of pure punching power I ever witnessed.

Not so impressive was Foreman's boorish behavior afterwards. The new champion seemed intent on making himself the most unpopular athlete in the world. He started out his first press conference as champion by announcing that no one was allowed to speak unless he gave them his regal permission. The morning after the fight, I saw Foreman in the Sheraton lobby and extended my hand to congratulate him. He brusquely pushed it aside and walked away. Big George might occupy the throne of Dempsey, Tunney, Louis, Marciano, and now Frazier, but George wasn't anywhere near their league when it came to class. However, I'm happy to say that the big fellow outgrew such behavior.

Following his tremendous victory against Frazier, Foreman scored two crushing knockouts in defense of his title, the last against the highly regarded Ken Norton. But the cloak of invincibility draped around George's massive shoulders was snatched away by Muhammad Ali in their "Rumble in the Jungle," just twenty months after he won the championship. The "Old Master" proved to the world that the big lug had as many flaws as strengths by knocking him out in the eighth round of what was as stunning and implausible an upset as Ali's first victory over Sonny Liston more than ten years earlier.

Foreman scored a string of knockouts on the comeback trail but then suffered another devastating defeat at the hands of wily Jimmy Young. In his dressing room afterwards, George underwent some sort of religious conversion and for the next decade spent his time preaching instead of punching. Then, in 1987, the now bald-headed, Buddahesque Foreman, announced his return to the ring. The paunch was not the only thing different about George; his personality had undergone a sea change, too. The surly, bent-on-destruction monster was gone, and in his place was a charismatic, cheeseburger-loving, talk-show host's dream. He even seemed apologetic about knocking guys out.

His first few comeback fights did little to discourage his critics, of whom I was one. But George steadily improved, and the fight crowd noticed that the old guy, while not the dreadnought of past years, could still really sock. His style was more deliberate and relaxed than the young, overanxious Foreman, who lusted for total annihilation in the shortest possible time. His winning back the heavyweight championship by beating Michael Moorer is one of sport's modern miracles.

From street thug to flag-waving Olympic hero, from the menacing Darth Vader persona of his first championship reign to the beloved and benevolent ancient warrior the second time around, Big George Foreman's life was quite an odyssey as well as a great American story. In the American cult of reinventing oneself, nobody did it better than this punching preacher who was born again—and again and again.

chapter 23

IN THE MAELSTROM

A FTER HIS LOSS to Joe Frazier, Ali beat Jimmy Ellis, Buster Mathis, George Chuvalo and several others in a virtual round-the-world tour. In September 1972, he was back at the Garden against two-time former Heavyweight Champion Floyd Patterson. Seven years earlier, Patterson had lost to Ali in a title match that some likened to watching a fly get his wings pulled off. Ali tortured Floyd because the former champion insisted on calling him by what Ali considered his former slave name: Cassius Clay.

Now Floyd was almost thirty-eight but still as popular as ever. The fight was a sellout. New Yorkers not only admired the Brooklyn native's boxing skill but also cottoned to his sportsmanship, graciousness and gentlemanly manner. I always said myself that if you don't like Floyd Patterson, you don't like people. Of course, having Ali in the other corner didn't exactly hurt ticket sales, either.

Patterson's strategy was to have Ali come to him, which, according to Floyd's blueprint, would let him control the tempo of the fight by picking his spots. Such tactics seemed counterintuitive, since the conventional wisdom always had been that the way to beat Ali was to crowd him. That's what I always believed. Give Ali room and he'd perform miracles.

At the bell Ali came out as if he was going for a stroll in the park. Patterson, keeping with his strategy, waited for Ali to come to him. Floyd still had those fast hands and he would, on occasion, score with a cluster of punches. Ali seemed unfazed by it all, almost supremely indifferent, as if just biding his time.

This went on for the first few rounds, and even though Floyd was doing pretty well, one always had the feeling that Ali was just waiting for the right moment to lower the boom. The crowd, though, was with Floyd, and you could tell that he was buoyed by their support.

In the middle rounds Ali began to open up, and by the seventh Patterson's eye was in a ghastly state. He was being repeatedly tattooed by stinging punches, and it was pointless to let it go on. I stopped the fight before the bell sounded for round eight. Patterson bravely protested, but the fans agreed with the stoppage. Patterson was a beloved figure; no one wanted to see him hurt. I was happy to learn later that Floyd decided to retire.

Before Patterson was seriously cut, some at ringside thought he was actually ahead until the stoppage. I was not one of them. Patterson never regained the form and fury that he showed in recapturing the title from Ingemar Johansson twelve years earlier. And even if he could, Patterson never had a prayer of winning against a Muhammad Ali. Ali's blend of size and speed would have always been too much for Patterson—who physically was no heavyweight. Frankly, I didn't even think he was a full-fledged light heavyweight; he always seemed to me more like a big middleweight.

I once mentioned this publicly and was upset to learn that Patterson was offended by my remarks. I later explained to Floyd that my comments were by no means demeaning but were really meant as a compliment: despite his physical disadvantages, his great skills and fighting heart enabled him to win the heavyweight title twice, the first man ever to accomplish that feat. Floyd seemed to understand—I think.

Refereeing the Ali–Patterson fight was a breeze. There was no controversy and no second-guessing of my decision to stop the fight. If only it could be this way with every fight. Controversy is not only part of boxing, at times it seems downright married to it. During my career

I've certainly had my share of it. One of my most publicized controversies was the third Muhammad Ali–Ken Norton fight, which I refereed in Yankee Stadium in September 1976.

Interest in the fight was very high since it was the rubber match of their famed trilogy. Norton had upset Ali in their first fight by winning a split decision, and Ali took the rematch also by split decision. Norton gave Ali fits both times, actually breaking his jaw in the first fight. An enormous and unruly crowd packed Yankee Stadium to see number three.

Like their first two bouts, this one was very close. For the first time, I could see how much Ali had deteriorated as a fighter. Throughout the course of the fight, he tended to rely more on tricks than boxing skills, doing more clinching than punching. Nevertheless, the two judges scored it eight rounds to seven for Ali, and I gave it to him on a vote of 8-6-1. The reaction of the spectators told me the decision was not popular. The people who thought Norton won harkened back to the first Joe Louis–Jersey Joe Walcott fight when it seemed the champion got the decision because he *was* the champion. In their minds, Ali was given the decision based on who he was rather than what he did in the ring that night.

The result soon snowballed into a huge public controversy. Accusations and counteraccusations were flung about with total disregard for the truth; there were angry demands for an investigation, and loose tongues questioned the motives of the officials absent of any evidence to support those charges. It was ugly.

You have no idea what it is like to be in the middle of a controversy of this magnitude until you experience it firsthand. It's like the eyes of the world are focused exclusively on you, and in the heat of the media circus it feels like 200 degrees in the shade.

Despite the mounting pressure, I kept cool. At a press conference at Gallagher's Steakhouse, the fight judges and I discussed why we scored it the way we did. I made no apologies, and vigorously defended my verdict. I relayed to the reporters that before the last round began I heard Angelo Dundee, Ali's trainer, screaming at his fighter that there were just three minutes left and he would have to fight like hell to hold on to his title.

Yelling just as vehemently was Norton's manager, Bob Biron, but unlike Dundee he was exhorting his fighter to take no chances in the final round because, as Biron saw it, Norton had the fight won. I thought that was just terrible advice. You never take anything for granted— especially the subjective scoring of a boxing match.

Taking my cue from Mark Twain—"Get the facts first; you can distort them later"—I suggested that since all three officials had Ali winning the conclusive last round and since many in the media had Norton winning it, it might be helpful to review the fifteenth round by isolating it into three discreet minutes. That was done, and the replay clearly showed Ali throwing more effective punches to win the final round.

Of course, one round, even the last one, does not make a fight. But because so many reporters who had scored the fifteenth round for Norton now changed their minds, I scored a psychological victory. If they were wrong about who won the fifteenth round, then they could be wrong about who won the fight.

The controversy seemed to be quelled. Not that everyone ended up agreeing with our decision, but because of our head-on approach they at least came to believe that even if the decision was not the right one, at least it was an honest one.

Shortly after that fight, I was riding the Long Island Railroad into Penn Station when I noticed a middle-aged, impeccably dressed man with sharp blue eyes staring at me. I fixed my eyes on my newspaper until he walked over, stuck out his hand and said, "You're the boxing referee Arthur Mercante."

When I asked if we knew each other, the fellow smiled and said, "Well, sir, you know nothing about me, but I know a great deal about you. Do you realize, sir," he continued with an exaggerated accent on his vowels, "that you are a bona fide celebrity—I mean a true-to-life bona fide celebrity?"

"Oh, come now," I started to demur.

But he cut me off: "No, sir, I'm quite serious about it. I know, because I write the obituaries for the *New York Times*—I mean, I write them in advance of a person's death so they will be ready at a moment's notice to go to print in the event of a celebrity's untimely demise.

"I know all about your career because just recently I wrote your obituary, and I must say, sir," he concluded, grabbing my hand again to shake it, "it's an honor, sir, a real honor to have written your obituary."

With that, he laughed heartily—a little too heartily, actually. A shot of Courvoisier would've done me some good right about then.

chapter 24

BLOW BY BLOW WITH HOWARD COSELL

I N THE SPRING of 1978, I had just finished making a speech at a sports dinner that was warmly received by the audience. I had no sooner made my way back to my seat when I felt a tap on my shoulder. It was Roone Arledge, president of the hugely successful ABC-TV Sports. Arledge was responsible for the critically acclaimed *Wide World of Sports* and the enormously popular *Monday Night Football*. He was a creator, a brilliant innovator, willing to experiment with new and bold ideas in television programming.

"You know, Arthur," Arledge said softly, "you have an excellent speaking voice. We are looking for a boxing analyst to work with Howard Cosell at the upcoming Ken Norton–Larry Holmes championship fight in Vegas that is going to be televised in prime time. I would like to assign you to work with Howard and producer Chet Forte. Do you think you might be interested?" I told him I was and that I had actually given some thought to the broadcasting booth. A handshake later and it was a done deal.

I looked forward to this new challenge. My good friend Gil Clancy, who had trained Welterweight and Middleweight Champion Emile Griffith, had made a brilliant transition from boxing trainer to analyst. I thought Gil brought a fresh and unique perspective to the broadcasting booth. I hoped to do the same from my experience as a boxing referee.

When I arrived, Las Vegas was hot, muggy and, as always, full of life. Over the last few years Vegas had replaced New York as the citadel of boxing, and by fight night the casinos were jumping and celebrities could be seen everywhere.

In the hotel lobby I spotted the loose-limbed, angular frame of Howard Cosell, indisputably the most recognized face and voice in sports broadcasting. He was called "The Mouth that Roared," and everything Howard did in broadcasting built upon that reputation. I had known Cosell for twenty years, and he came exactly as advertised: vain, verbose, self-absorbed and insufferable. Although I had always gotten along very well with him, there were many powerful and influential people in sports who hated his guts. When someone once remarked to renowned boxing publicist Irving Rudd that Howard was his own worst enemy, Rudd replied, "Not while I'm alive!"

While one could understand why the controversial, outspoken, self-proclaimed, "tell-it-like-it-is" Cosell made enemies, it was a mistake to underestimate his genuine talents. Armed with a superb vocabulary and a photographic memory, Cosell's inimitable style and unerring instinct for the dramatic made him a gifted performer and a natural broadcaster.

As always, Cosell greeted me with great fanfare. He always flattered me by calling me boxing's best referee. We spoke about the upcoming fight. I told him it was an interesting match-up that ought to spark interest in what was becoming a dull post–Muhammad Ali era. Both fighters were talented and deserving. Ken Norton had defeated the elusive Jimmy Young for recognition as World Boxing Council champion. He was awkwardly strong, a good puncher and for most boxers a very difficult man to fight.

Larry Holmes was a boxer, not a slugger, relying on finesse and speed rather than strength and raw power. He had come up the hard way. He had been embarrassed by Duane Bobick at the 1972 U.S. Olympic Trials and was accused of actually quitting in that fight. The charge was ludicrous—Holmes never quit in his life. He redeemed himself in the eyes of skeptics by winning twenty-seven straight fights as a pro, and no one could deny that he had exceptional boxing skills.

Cosell nodded as I spoke, and I thought things had gotten off to a good start. But as we were leaving the lobby, Cosell suddenly turned to me and said acidly, "You know, Arthur, I'm a professional announcer, and I don't need guys like you and Clancy to work with me. I've been broadcasting fights since the 1950s, and I'm perfectly capable of handling the broadcast by myself."

I was too shocked to respond. I knew Cosell had been critical of ex-jocks as sports broadcasters, but I didn't realize his hostility also included referees and trainers behind the mike. It was an omen of things to come.

Later, I became even more disturbed when I learned that a production meeting was held and I wasn't even invited. There seemed to be a deliberate attempt to marginalize my role in the upcoming broadcast. No one briefed me nor made any effort to give me any direction. Production people began to avoid me. It was a lousy feeling. I tried to seek out Roone Arledge to ask him what the hell was going on, but he was nowhere to be found. I was on my own.

On the night of the fight, I was fitted into a blue sports blazer with the ABC logo emblazoned on the pocket. I sat at ringside with Cosell, who spent his pre-fight time greeting well-wishers and jawboning about the deplorable state of boxing. Howard, as the world knew, was enthralled by the sound of his nasally voice. He totally ignored me, and I was resigned to just sitting, watching the Caesars Palace arena fill to capacity.

Finally, Howard gave me the honor of addressing me: "Arthur, all you have to do is follow my lead. During the fight I'll ask you some questions that you will answer forthrightly and honestly. If you see something worth noting about the fight, feel free to comment on it." Then he told me to pay particular attention to a button on the control panel in front of me. "This button controls your mike," he said.

"When I press it you are not on the air, when I release it, you're on. It's that simple."

The two fighters entered the ring. At six foot three inches both fighters were exactly the same height with more or less the same reach. That is where the similarities ended. At 209 pounds, Holmes looked svelte and smoothly muscled, whereas Norton, with his 220 perfectly proportioned muscular pounds, looked like Mr. Olympia with boxing gloves on.

As they moved to the center of the ring for instructions, Holmes sought to stare Norton down. I never thought much of this staring business—fights are won with fists, not stares. Both fighters towered over referee Mills Lane.

Howard Cosell noted to the television audience at home that Arthur Mercante, famous for refereeing the second Patterson–Johansson and first Ali–Frazier fights, was at ringside and would be offering his observations from time to time.

The bell sounded for the first round. Following Cosell's instructions, I tried to comment on the action but was quickly rebuffed. It soon became clear that Cosell intended to monopolize the entire broadcast. He would either shush me or rapidly tap me on the knee to convey that my input was not welcome. When there was a pause in the action, he would push the "off" button and ask me what I was going to say. With his finger on the button, only Howard could hear my remarks.

He would nod vigorously and then, to my profound consternation, would repeat my observations to the nationwide audience as if they were his own. His only half-hearted attempt at attribution came when, after repeating one of my observations, he intoned, "And Arthur Mercante agrees with me."

I wanted to get up and scream, "No, Howard, you lying son of a bitch, I'm not agreeing with you—you're agreeing with me!" But we were on the air, and there wasn't a damn thing I could do about it except sit there, smoldering.

One of the things I noticed was what a magnificent left jab Larry Holmes possessed. I always knew he had a good jab, but I never truly appreciated its greatness until that evening. The left jab is boxing's purest punch, and to see it executed so masterfully is exhilarating to anyone who appreciates the science of boxing. Holmes's jab was a millisecond slower than Ali's in his prime, but it was just as accurate and even more punishing. Behind that left jab, Holmes dominated the early rounds of a fast-paced fight.

As the fight proceeded into the middle rounds, I tried more aggressively to do what I was being paid for—provide analysis for the fight. Cosell, however, parried beautifully. Instead of just shushing me or tapping me on the knee to shut me up, he now resorted to keeping his finger on the "off" button. Howard was fighting dirty, but there was no referee to stop him from hitting below the belt.

The middle rounds saw the tide of the fight turning in Ken Norton's favor as his strength, rather than Holmes's boxing skills, began to dictate the action. Norton was beginning to hammer home some powerful punches, and Holmes could no longer keep him at bay. It was a hell of a fight.

Incredibly, the tide turned once again, as Holmes roared back with blistering combinations. All the years of struggling to the top had created an inner toughness that would not be denied. Holmes was not an Olympic champion, nor a media star; he had to claw his way to the top. This was his big chance, maybe his only chance. He was not about to blow it.

Holmes scored big in the thirteenth round. Norton was on the verge of being knocked out, but then Ken, too, reached for something deep inside and refused to fall. This is the stuff great fights are made of and, if Ali–Frazier IV would never be, this war in Vegas was the next best thing to it.

By the fifteenth and final round, both fighters should have been completely spent. Yet they stood toe-to-toe slugging it out. The sell-out crowd screamed their lungs out as the momentum of the fight swung back and forth, first to one fighter and then the other. I could only marvel in frustrated silence. That fifteenth round was one for the ages—it was simply the best finale I ever saw. If I had realized earlier this fight would become one of the best heavyweight title matches in the last fifty years, I would have been even more disturbed by having been rendered almost mute by the ludicrous insecurities of an egocentric broadcaster.

Holmes was declared the new Heavyweight Champion of the World by virtue of a split decision. Norton was bitterly disappointed, but, as always, faced defeat like a man. I always liked that about Norton: he walked tall.

After that epic fight, Ken Norton lost as often as he won. Finally, he suffered a brutal knockout in fifty-four seconds of the first round by Gerry Cooney. It was the fastest knockout for a main event in the history of Madison Square Garden.

Later, a cub reporter, remembering that Kenny was also knocked out early by George Foreman, asked Norton, "Who hits harder, Ken, Gerry Cooney or George Foreman?"

Norton answered with delicious sarcasm, "I don't know, kid, I didn't have my gauge on me."

You have to love a guy who, even in the face of disaster, can keep his sense of humor.

Larry Holmes would rule the roost for seven years and defend his title an astonishing twenty-one times, second only to the incomparable Joe Louis. For all that, Holmes never got his just due as champion. Like Gene Tunney, who succeeded Jack Dempsey, and Ezzard Charles after Joe Louis, Holmes could never escape the gigantic shadow of his predecessor, Muhammad Ali, and unfortunately Holmes, a person of quality, could not conceal his bitterness. So much of life is timing, and the sad lesson for these ring greats is that a living legend is just that, it never dies but lives on forever.

As for me, I didn't dwell on my disappointment with my foray into TV broadcasting or hold any grudges. Whenever I saw Howard Cosell after that, I was always cordial to him. I found out long ago that hurts are like babies—the more you nurse them, the bigger they get, and ultimately you end up hurting no one but yourself. A career in big-time boxing broadcasting wasn't in the cards, but as the 1980s rolled into view and I entered my sixth decade of refereeing fights, there was still plenty to look forward to. And, doing what I did best, it was easy to chalk up my brush with TV broadcasting to experience as I got ready to answer the bell for the next round.

chapter 25
LONG ISLAND'S WHITE HOPE

O NE OF THE differences between professional boxing and sports such as baseball, football or basketball is that boxing doesn't hold tryouts. A fan going to see a major league baseball game or an NBA game is guaranteed to see athletes performing their craft with a certain level of skill. Those who lack the ability to play at that level have long ago been weeded out of the system.

Boxing, however, is a horse of an altogether different color. All that is required to fight professionally is to pass the physical. A clean bill of health virtually assures a professional license. The upshot is a lot of fighters competing with marginal skills and, worse still, ill-conditioned boxers and mismatches with potentially dangerous outcomes.

In the 1970s and '80s I ran a boxing program on Long Island for the Township of Hempstead. It was an enormously successful program that was very popular with the boys and men who participated. Some of them went on to compete in the Golden Gloves, and several even won championships.

Winning titles, however, was of secondary importance. I purposely designed the program to be more than just learning about hooks and jabs. I have always believed that the discipline of boxing puts a premium on a sound and fit body, builds character and self-confidence, and inspires manly courage. It was these values, above all, that I sought to impart to the young men who enrolled in my program.

Except for those I thought exceptional, I generally discouraged our boys from even entering Golden Gloves competition. I tried to be as diplomatic as possible with them because, having raised four sons, I knew how tender the male ego could be. But there were always those desperate for a sense of self-worth who figured that boxing was the pathway to that end. To them I explained that just by completing our rigorous regimen they had become success stories, worthy of honor and self-respect. There was nothing further to prove by swapping punches in competition. Most of the kids abided by my counsel, but sometimes my advice was no match for dreams of ring glory.

Randy Gordon was a boxing junkie who joined one of my classes. While he picked up the fundamentals of boxing well enough he, to put it kindly, lacked the ability to execute them with any effectiveness. But he was an earnest and likable enough kid, so I made him an instructor, thinking it best to keep him outside the ring as much as possible rather than inside, where I felt he was in jeopardy even during friendly sparring matches.

One day Randy came to me all flushed with excitement. "Mr. Mercante, I've got some good news," he said. "I got my professional boxing license, and I'm fighting on the undercard of the Cooney–Lyle fight at the Nassau Coliseum."

I couldn't believe what I was hearing. Randy had no business in the Golden Gloves, much less fighting as a professional. "You did what?" I said.

"I got my pro boxing license," he repeated proudly.

"You got your . . . Randy, listen to me, please." When I tried to tell him, as gently as possible, that he was making a terrible mistake, he got very defensive and finally tried to mollify me by telling me his opponent was a "stiff" who wouldn't give him any trouble.

"Look, Randy, I don't want to hurt your feelings, but I have to level with you. I don't care who you are fighting, you're not pro material."

But there was no talking to him. I decided I was going to speak with

Jim Farley, chairman of the NYSAC, and have his license revoked. I usually don't intrude in other people's business, but this seemed to be a matter of life and death. I didn't want to see the kid get hurt. Since he had gotten his start in my boxing program, I felt a sense of responsibility. I had to do something; I didn't want blood on my hands.

The next morning I called Jim Farley and told him to revoke Gordon's license. On what grounds? Farley wanted to know. "On the grounds that he is likely to get himself killed!" I exclaimed.

"That's just your opinion, Arthur," Farley shot back. If Gordon passed the physical, the chairman emphatically explained, he qualified for a professional boxer's license, and to revoke it would leave the commission open to a discrimination lawsuit.

Talking to Farley was like talking to Gordon. I couldn't help thinking that this kid might really get hurt, and boxing needs another black eye like I need to do another televised broadcast with Howard Cosell.

Farley, however, was the last court of appeal. As you get older, you become more accepting of the fact that there are some things you have no control over. But my warning must have registered with Farley because an hour or so later he called me back.

"Arthur, I got some good news. I checked that Gordon thing out, and he is fighting a kid who is a nothing, a real tomato can. Why, he might even win!" he said, laughing.

"Win!" I said, stunned at the very idea. "Jim, I don't care how inept the other guy is, I'm telling you, Gordon can't lick a postage stamp!"

"Well, that's the best I could do!" Farley bellowed, his voice suddenly very angry. "You want me to get my ass sued off?"

As fate would have it, I was assigned to referee the Gerry Cooney–Ron Lyle fight and was ringside as the timekeeper for Randy Gordon's professional debut. Gordon entered the ring, looking something like Dick Cavett in boxing trunks. Somehow Randy made it through the first round. When the bell rang for the second, he came out again and made a few more feeble gestures at the "Manly Art" before the tomato can poleaxed him with such dispatch and finality that it was shocking. Randy Gordon lay prostrate on the canvas, oblivious to all around him. It was beyond pathetic; Gordon was out, and I was afraid he was hurt seriously, maybe even fatally.

C'mon Randy, I said to myself. *Show me you're alive; move a finger, a toe, anything*. But he just lay there motionless. As they brought him out on a stretcher, a pall of silence enveloped the arena. Following Gordon and the paramedics out, I ran into a distraught Jim Farley full of remorse. "I should have listened to you, Arthur, I should have listened to you," he fairly keened.

No sense going through the "I told you so routine." While Randy was being attended to, I returned to the ring to referee the main event between Cooney and Lyle.

As it turned out, it didn't even go as long as the Gordon affair. In the first round, Cooney, who could really bang, bulled Lyle to the ropes and fired off several howitzer left hooks that fractured a couple of ribs and sent Lyle sprawling halfway outside the ropes. It was a tremendously impressive performance even if Lyle was all washed up as a heavyweight contender. Clearly, Cooney was a rising star and a genuine threat to Heavyweight Champion Larry Holmes. This kid was no mere hyped-up White Hope; he was big, fast and had a left hook like a high-powered pile driver that broke bones like they were matchsticks.

Cooney's left hook to the body reminded me of Joe Baksi, a burly heavyweight contender in the 1940s. But where Baksi could hurt you with his left, the 6½-foot Irishman could literally kill you with it. The fact that Cooney's right was only good for shaking hands really didn't matter much. That crushing left hook was his ticket to stardom, since boxing fans are always hungry for a heavyweight with a big punch.

As Cooney and I were from Long Island, I had taken a keen interest in the big Irishman's career from the Golden Gloves on. I liked to

George Foreman floored Joe Frazier six times during their World Heavyweight Championship fight in Kingston, Jamaica, January 1973. I stopped the fight in the second round.

A youthful Denny Moyer takes on 41-year-old Sugar Ray Robinson, February 1962. Moyer won by a 10-round decision.

My uncle Joe Monte was a professional boxer. He fought Max Schmeling and took on James J. Braddock three times.

I enlisted in the U.S. Navy in 1942 and got my first taste of refereeing when I officiated at boxing matches between recruits.

A victorious Roy Jones Jr. accepts the adulation of the crowd after beating Montell Griffin for the World Light Heavyweight Championship, August 1997.

JAN. 1, 1973 - KINGSTON, JAMAICA
HEAVYWEIGHT CHAMPIONSHIP of WORLD
GEORGE FOREMAN vs JOE FRAZIER
FOREMAN winner and new Champion
T.K.O. 2nd RD. - REFEREE:
ARTHUR L. MERCANTE

What a way to start the new year! George Foreman wins the Heavyweight Championship of the World in Kingston, Jamaica, January 1, 1973.

World Heavyweight Championship
Muhammad Ali vs Kenny Norton #3
Yankee Stadium 9/28/76
Winner: Muhammad Ali 15 Round Decision
Referee: Arthur L. Mercante

Kenny Norton connects with a straight left to Muhammad Ali during the World Heavyweight Championship fight in Yankee Stadium, September 1976. Ali won by a 15-round decision.

My friend Anthony Quinn and I chat on the set of *Requiem for a Heavyweight.*

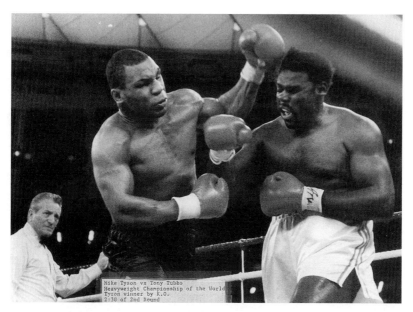

Mike Tyson and Tony Tubbs trade blows for the Heavyweight Championship of the World in Tokyo, March 1988. Tyson won by a knockout.

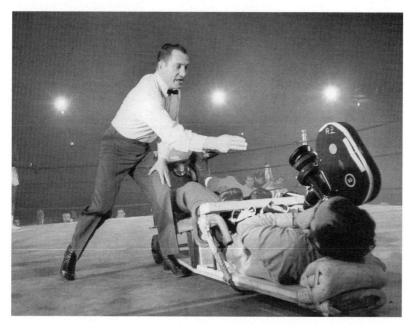

In the Hollywood movie *Requiem for a Heavyweight*, the camera man had to lie on a dolly to catch the action as I gave washed-up heavyweight contender "Mountain Rivera" the ten-count.

I've shared fifty-two fantastic years of marriage with my wonderful wife, Gloria..

I am blessed to have four terrific sons (l to r): Arthur Jr., James, Glenn, and Tom (That's me in the middle.)

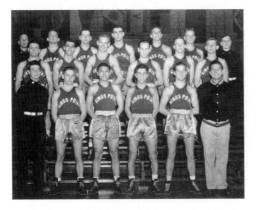

I coached the U.S. Merchant Marine Academy boxing team after leaving the navy. In the first year, 1947, three members went to the national championship!

Roy Jones Jr. and David Telesco go at it before a packed Radio City Music Hall audience, January 2000. Roy won by unanimous decision.

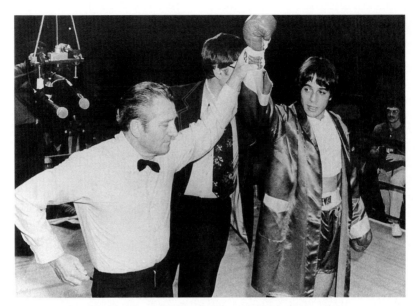

Tony Danza wins over Max Hord by a knockout, April 1979. Shortly afterwards, the multitalented Tony decided to give up boxing to pursue acting full time. He became a good friend.

Ingemar Johansson is out on the canvas, and Floyd Patterson is about to regain the Heavyweight Championship of the World, June 1960.

follow the careers of some of the fighters who came from my backyard. I liked Levittown's Bobby Cassidy, the tough middleweight–light heavyweight contender, who was a real scrapper. I even got to referee some of Bobby's fights.

But Gerry Cooney was high profile. He was a heavyweight, he was white and he was just demolishing guys. He was unquestionably the greatest heavyweight to ever come out of the Island, which, I suppose, is a little bit like being the tallest skyscraper in Wichita, Kansas. But Cooney was the real thing—no one seemed able to last more than a few rounds with him, and after he dramatically, damn near fatally, annihilated Ken Norton in fifty-four dramatic seconds, he looked destined to be the next heavyweight king.

There were, however, two major problems obstructing his ascent to heavyweight laurels. Problem number one was that Larry Holmes was the champion he had to dethrone—a tall order. Problem number two was that Cooney did not seem to really have the heart for boxing. Raised in a working middle-class family, he seemed to lack the hunger that is an essential ingredient for most would-be champions. In fact, Cooney's most compelling motivation was to win the title for his deceased father, whose dream had been to see Gerry become champion. A noble aspiration for sure, but boxing is the toughest game in the world, and you had better dream your own dreams and not live someone else's.

Cooney did eventually get his crack at the championship and acquitted himself honorably in his title match against Holmes. Despite being knocked down in the second round, Cooney made it a competitive fight all the way and gave the champion some real anxious moments. But ultimately Holmes's boxing ability and know-how prevailed, and Cooney's bid ended in the thirteenth round. Holmes called Cooney the toughest of all his challengers, and it seemed only a matter of time before Gerry would regroup and become champion.

But Cooney rarely fought again, and in his infrequent appearances he did not perform inspiringly. Finally, "Gentleman Gerry" succumbed to the numbing power of George Foreman's sledgehammers, and the Cooney odyssey was over for good.

As for poor Randy Gordon, he woke up from his deep snooze to make a full recovery. To my great relief and boxing's everlasting gratitude, he never fought again. I always felt that Randy's self-imposed retirement was his greatest contribution to the advancement of our sport. Gordon would later make hay of his pugilistic debacle by writing an article entitled, "What It Feels Like to Be Knocked Out." There was no finer authority. Both as a boxer and later as chairman of the New York State Athletic Commission, Gordon's proven ability to achieve a complete state of unconsciousness was beyond dispute.

chapter 26

SUGAR RAY LEONARD
and the little fellers

A SIDE FROM THE ascent of heavyweight Gerry Cooney, attention started to drift away from the heavyweights, and the spotlight began to shine on the much-neglected lighter divisions that were ripe with talent. This especially was the case in the 147-pound welterweight class, which then featured such outstanding performers as former Champion Carlos Palomino, the brilliant young Champion Wilfred Benitez, a two-handed bomber named Pipino Cuevas and a young, tall, raw-boned gunslinger called Tommy "Hit Man" Hearns. But the division really got a jolt of electricity when legendary Lightweight Champion Roberto Duran, called "Manos de Piedra" or "Hands of Stone," moved up to welterweight at the same time charismatic gold medal Olympic Champion Sugar Ray Leonard was carving out a reputation for himself in that same division.

Duran was frequently dubbed "pound for pound" the best fighter in the world, and he may have been. The ferocious, hard-hitting Panamanian fought not only with demonic intensity, he was what we call in the business a real "cutie." He knew all the tricks. From the slums of Panama, Duran punched his way to ring stardom. There was a magnetism in his fury and demeanor—his eyes were like dark coals and his heart seemed to smolder with the cinders of Hell. Heavyweight contender Jerry Quarry once told me that despite their size difference he would dread the thought of having to fight Duran in some broken-down saloon. The Panamanian ruffian was truly a menacing figure in or out of the ring.

There were some who even claimed Duran was the greatest lightweight ever. Not quite. I never saw Benny Leonard, but "Manos de Piedra" would have had his hands full against greats I did see like Tony Canzoneri, Barney Ross, Ike Williams and Hank Armstrong. "Hammerin' Hank" was so good that he won the welterweight title while weighing only 133½ pounds and held three different titles simultaneously back in the days when there were only eight overall, not a veritable buffet selection of titles like today.

Even if Duran was not quite the greatest, there is no denying he was one little package of dynamite. In his first seventy-three professional fights he only lost once. That was against Esteban DeJesus in 1972, a fight I refereed. It was the first time anyone ever put Duran on the canvas, which DeJesus did, courtesy of a left hook in the first round. After ten rounds of hard fighting, I raised the right hand of DeJesus in victory. It was a non-title fight. Later in two title defenses Duran, bent on revenge, KO'd DeJesus twice.

And then along came Sugar Ray Leonard. Leonard was one of five gold medal winners for the U.S.A. in the 1976 Olympics, and I could see he was the most gifted fighter of that remarkable bunch. He fought in the 139-pound division, and I thought with proper management this could be the fighter to challenge Duran's dominance. Some pooh-poohed him as just a media creation, but Leonard proved them wrong by impressively defeating everyone he faced, including the gifted Wilfred Benitez to win the Welterweight Championship of the World on a fifteenth-round stoppage.

The drums began to beat loudly for a Duran–Leonard showdown, a fight fan's dream if there ever was one. The ballyhoo for that exceeded anything I ever saw in boxing except for the most celebrated of heavyweight championship matches.

But before Leonard could fight Duran, he signed for a title defense against Davey "Boy" Green of Great Britain in Landover, Maryland—right in Ray's backyard. Green was a moderately talented fighter known for his gameness more than anything else. I got the assignment to referee the fight.

I went to ringside where I began my routine of bouncing up and down on the canvas, checking the tightness of the ring ropes and just looking around for anything out of order or just plain unusual. Just like a fighter, a referee needs to prepare himself. I tried to eliminate as many surprises as I could before the bell even rang. A fight will bring you surprises enough without the ropes and ring posts collapsing because somebody didn't do his job properly.

Before the fight, I went into each fighter's dressing room and reviewed the rules. I had something more in mind for Ray Leonard, though. I had noticed that in some of his previous fights, Leonard had adopted some of the antics of Muhammad Ali. Ali's influence was so large on young, impressionable fighters that many felt they had to copy everything he did. How many fighters did I see get creamed because they tried, like the former champion, to rope-a-dope an opponent?

I never liked playfulness in the ring. Boxing is a serious and dangerous business. I did not tolerate these antics with Ali, and I was not going to start with Leonard. When I entered his dressing room, Ray's renowned trainer, Angelo Dundee, who of course had also trained Ali, was taping Ray's hands.

After reviewing the rules with the champion, I looked him square in the eye and said, "Ray, you don't have to imitate Ali. Forget about the 'Ali Shuffle,' the 'Rope-a-Dope,' the 'Anchor Punch' and all that other stuff. You're a great talent, Ray, a great fighter. You don't have to be another Ali; all you have to be is Ray Leonard. So I'm telling you now, right here in this dressing room, that I don't want any nonsense. Do I make myself clear, Champ?"

Leonard nodded affirmatively, and as I was leaving the dressing room, Dundee came up and whispered, "Thanks, Art, I've been telling him that for months, but the kid just won't listen to me."

As I called the fighters to the center of the ring it was Davey "Boy" Green who tried to intimidate Ray Leonard. He was staring bullets at Ray, and Leonard responded in kind. Give this to Green—he had guts.

What he didn't have were the skills to cope with Leonard's great ability. The hand speed, the lateral movement, the timing—Ray had the whole package. I was right: he didn't need showboating to brighten his spotlight. After three rounds, Ray was clearly ahead, but Green was unhurt and still willing. Despite the deficit in talent, the Brit was doing better than I expected.

The most frightening thing about boxing is that the violence can be so swift a bout can end with almost revolting suddenness. A fighter can be strong and vigorous one moment, and then the next reduced to a senseless heap of flesh on the canvas. That's what happened to Green in round four.

Leonard, an underrated puncher, felled him with a blinding combination that seemed to come out of nowhere. Those trigger-fast reflexes were never more in evidence. Davey Boy fell like a guy going through a trap door, and I feared he was seriously hurt. But smelling salts and cold compresses brought him around again.

Leonard's showdown with Duran happened a few months later, in June 1980. After fifteen furiously fought rounds, Leonard suffered the first loss of his career. But if there's such a thing as a moral victory, it was Ray's because he proved beyond all doubt that it was sheer grit that brought him the distance against one of ringdom's most ferocious fighters.

Just five months later, Leonard got his revenge by making Duran, the very symbol of machismo, inexplicably quit in the infamous "No mas, No mas" fight—a night that will live in boxing infamy. By quitting the way he did, Duran literally flushed a legendary reputation right down the toilet. Later, he would partially redeem himself by winning the junior middleweight and middleweight belts. No ring glory, however, would ever fully eradicate the stench of his surrender.

In Thomas "Hit Man" Hearns, who scored a two-round knockout over Pipino Cuevas to win the World Boxing Association's welterweight title, Leonard had another natural rival. Hearns was quick-fisted, rangy and exceptionally tall for a welterweight. He also hit as hard as any 147-pounder that ever lived—harder than Baby-Faced Jimmy McLarnin or Tony DeMarco, and maybe as hard as Ray Robinson. This would be a real test for Leonard. He would be giving up height, reach and punching power to a fighter whose combinations were almost as swift as his own.

In the best welterweight title fight since the Carmen Basilio–Tony DeMarco bouts in the '50s, Leonard came from behind to knock out Hearns in the fourteenth round. It was a sensational win, and Ray Leonard was acclaimed one of the greatest fighters of his era and one of the best welterweights of all time.

Soon after the Hearns bout, a detached retina forced Ray into his first retirement. Few champions stay retired, though, and Leonard would make several comebacks over the next few years. In 1987, after a three-year hiatus, Ray proved there was still some magic in his fists when he scored an improbable victory over Marvin Hagler to win the Middleweight Championship of the World. But like so many others, he went on too long and embarrassed himself in his last fight with Hector Camacho, in 1997, when his legs just failed him.

How good was he at his best? It's hard to say. How do you compare a champion who had just over forty professional fights with one who had over two hundred fights? I put Leonard in the same category as a Sandy Koufax, a Pistol Pete Reiser or a Gale Sayers. They were all marvelously gifted athletes with almost limitless potential, but their greatness has to be qualified because injuries prevented them from achieving dominance over a sustained period of time.

While he wasn't quite the greatest "Sugar" ever, Ray Leonard added a big dose of sweet to the Sweet Science. It was a privilege to be the third man in the ring whenever he had the gloves on.

chapter 27

IRON MIKE

THERE IS AN old saying in boxing: As the heavyweight division goes, so goes boxing. There is a lot of truth in that, and in the mid-1980s, both experienced what could only be described as a fistic tsunami caused by a reign of terror initiated by a man-child named Mike Tyson. A knockout artist extraordinaire, Tyson's boyishly menacing presence was the talk of the entire sports world.

In March 1986, an already famous Tyson made his Nassau County, Long Island, debut at the coliseum against a journeyman heavyweight named Steve Zouski. That it was taking place in my very backyard was welcome news, and I had high hopes I would get the assignment to referee the fight.

I knew Tyson was a hot commodity, but I didn't realize the magnitude of it until he and his entourage arrived. Though only nineteen, Mike was already receiving more media coverage than any other athlete since Muhammad Ali. When I got the call to referee the fight, I immediately found myself smack in the middle of a media feeding frenzy.

So intrigued were people by Tyson that everywhere I went I was bombarded with questions: Do you think he will be the next heavyweight champion? Will he beat Floyd Patterson's record of being the youngest heavyweight champion ever? How does he compare with the all-time greats?

The questions were endless. My stock response was only that Tyson showed great promise, but it was too early to tell. Which was the absolute truth. After all, I must have seen a thousand kids with real possibilities go to pieces once the going got tough. The fact remained that while Tyson was mopping up everyone they put before him, the kid really hadn't been tested in the ring.

Steve Zouski, a highway engineer from Wisconsin, was no big test, but even so interest in the fight was sky-high. The media and the fans were treating each Tyson fight as if it were a championship match. He had already been on the cover of *Sports Illustrated,* and his last fight, a knockout over Jesse Ferguson, was broadcast on ABC-TV's *Wide World of Sports.*

Like Jack Dempsey, whom Tyson admired and tried to emulate (he even had his head shaved in the Dempsey style), Tyson's mass appeal was rooted in the public's perception of him as a cold-blooded man-killer. Going into the Zouski fight, Tyson had won all eighteen of his professional fights by KO—twelve of them in the first round. Mike Tyson was looked upon as an untamed force of nature; much like one would view the power of a hurricane or a tornado, people were awed by the destruction he left in his wake. Even non-boxing fans were intrigued by his brand of unmitigated violence.

Thanks to a skilled public relations campaign launched by his savvy handlers, people were also drawn to the human side of the Tyson story. A product of the slums of Brownsville, Brooklyn, young Tyson was an incorrigible youth, apparently destined for a life of crime. Sent to reform school at the age of twelve, Tyson discovered boxing as an outlet for his anger and aggression. The boy's power and strength astonished his instructors. The pugilistic prodigy was brought to the attention of Cus D'Amato, and the aged, legendary trainer came out of retirement to take Tyson under his wing, molding him into a man, then a champion.

This tale took some liberties with the truth, but the essentials were mostly there. The white-haired D'Amato, who had brought Floyd Patterson and José Torres to world championships, spoke in fatherly tones, and with his homespun philosophy using boxing as a metaphor for life, he was regarded by many as a wizened oracle of the sport. The story of the old man and the kid, one white, one black, made irresistible copy. Their relationship took on even greater pathos after D'Amato's untimely death in November 1985.

I entered the ring in Nassau Coliseum that evening on March 10, 1986, curious to get my first close-up look at this "enfant terrible." The arena, not surprisingly, was sold out. The national sports media could be seen everywhere you looked.

Tyson entered the ring sockless and in black trunks. He vigorously twitched his head side-to-side to stretch that thick slab of muscle he called his neck. I could see right away that he wasn't within an inch of the five-feet-eleven-inches-tall his biography claimed, but the youngster was built like a fireplug. It was hard to believe a nineteen-year-old athlete could achieve such muscular development so young. As we waited for the ring announcer to make the introductions, Tyson just seemed to smolder in his corner. Everything about him conveyed menace and raw power.

Steve Zouski, on the other hand, had a fleshy, billowy look to him. With his squat, stout physique, Zouski reminded me of British heavyweight Don Cockell, who won the hearts of boxing fans by putting up an heroic, though futile, stand against Rocky Marciano in their 1955 title fight.

But Zouski wasn't even a Cockell who, despite his heft, could box and move. Zouski's style was such that you could not avoid hitting him. For all that, he had never been off his feet in the ring; so whatever limitations Zouski had in power and boxing skills, there was no shortage of courage and resoluteness. I made a mental note to watch him carefully. A referee has to be especially attentive to those resilient types, whose courage sometimes becomes a liability to their own well-being.

For two rounds Tyson showcased his blistering combinations. While I never cared for the peek-a-boo style inculcated by D'Amato, Tyson's frightening power and the speed of his combinations were for real. When Tyson unleashed, it was like the unfurling of an explosive burst of energy. Zouski, true to form, resisted destruction manfully, but by the third round he was just overwhelmed, and I stepped in to stop the slaughter. When I raised Tyson's powerful right arm in victory, the young man's pro career boasted nineteen straight knockouts—and no end in sight.

I didn't referee another Tyson fight for two more years. By then Tyson had won the heavyweight championship or at least the World Boxing Council's version and was a huge international celebrity. His worldwide appeal was one reason why Tyson's title defense against Tony Tubbs, once the WBA belt-holder, was to be held in Tokyo, Japan. It was the first heavyweight championship fight held in that country since George Foreman KO'd Joe "King" Roman fifteen years earlier.

Soon after I arrived in Narita Airport, I discovered that, like Americans, the Japanese people were utterly fascinated by Mike Tyson. He was mobbed by photographers and was a permanent fixture on Japanese television. The Japanese bestowed on him the almost god-like status usually reserved for their most celebrated sumo wrestlers. On the day fight tickets went on sale, an almost unheard of eighty percent of them were sold.

Meanwhile, amid an ocean of adulation, the tide of Tyson's personal life had become a soap opera. Iron Mike had married actress Robin Givens just three weeks earlier, and there was already talk about her tag-teaming with promoter Don King in an attempted coup against Tyson's managers, Bill Cayton and Jim Jacobs. Jacobs wasn't even in

Japan, and rumor put him in a New York hospital with a serious illness. It turned out to be all too tragically true, and two days after the fight, Jacobs passed away.

Against this backdrop of intrigue was the brewing mega-fight between Tyson and Spinks to unify the heavyweight title. Spinks had defeated Larry Holmes twice. This made Spinks the so-called linear heavyweight champion whose pedigree was traceable to the "Boston Strong Boy" himself, the great John L. Sullivan.

So once again, I found myself refereeing a fight that would set the stage for a super bout—and make no mistake about it, it is these fights that make a referee very uncomfortable. Nobody says it out loud, but in these cases the referee is not supposed to do anything to get in the way of the guy who is supposed to win.

As I entered the enormous, cavernous Tokyo Dome, dubbed the "Big Egg," I marveled at the quiet fashion in which 35,000 Japanese fans took their seats. I've seen noisier crowds at Sunday Mass. The Japanese truly are an extremely disciplined and restrained people.

Tubbs entered the ring first. Not known for his Spartan training habits, the challenger was offered a $50,000 bonus to come in no heavier than 235 pounds. But true to his name, Tubbs weighed in at a tubby 238. As he disrobed in his corner, I noted the jiggling blubber around his waistline. Why a young athlete with a $50,000 incentive, fighting for the richest prize in sports, cannot get himself in reasonable shape is beyond my comprehension. On the other hand, at 216 pounds, Tyson looked solid and ready.

As the bell sounded the first round, Tyson was looking to end the fight with one punch. This is always a mistake. Tubbs, an experienced fighter with a fair amount of natural ability, scored with left jabs and, surprisingly, some good body shots. I gave the first round to the challenger.

That would be all the glory Tony Tubbs would see that evening. In the second round, Tyson fought his way inside with a surprising series of left jabs. Once inside, Iron Mike banged away at Tubbs's ample midsection. Tubbs tried to fight back, but Tyson hit him harder and faster. I could hear Tubbs begin to wheeze with exhaustion when, thirty seconds before the round's end, Tyson landed a right hook to the body and followed it up with one of his signature uppercuts. The vicious punch snapped Tubbs's head violently back. As Tubbs reeled, Tyson landed a grazing left hook, but it was enough to put his already wobbling opponent down. Then, the champion almost blew it.

While Tubbs was sitting on the canvas, Tyson bent down and swung a powerful left at his head. It was a cold and deliberate attack on a hurt and helpless fighter. Fortunately for both of them, the punch missed. I say "fortunately" for Tyson, too, because if the blow had landed I would have immediately disqualified him without a thought to the Spinks match—a "no-no" in the mega-money world of championship boxing.

A disqualification of Tyson would undoubtedly have put me at the center of an enormous firestorm and under attack by an array of self-interested parties who cared nothing about boxing unless they could make a buck from it. Thankfully, it didn't come to that, and Tyson was still the heavyweight champion in the precincts of the globe under the sway of the WBC. But as someone once said, the rules are the rules.

On my long flight back to the States, I had a lot to think about. A great deal had happened, but my reverie was interrupted by the unmistakable sounds of a crap game. I was on the same flight home as the Tyson entourage, whose members were engaged in an animated dice game in the back of the plane. When I was in the navy, I shot a little dice myself. I left my seat and went back to join the fun.

Once there I saw a bundle of money in the middle of a circle of men as Kevin Rooney, Tyson's head trainer and an inveterate gambler, blew on the dice for luck. Just then a flight attendant interrupted the game to announce that gambling was not allowed on the plane. She was cheerfully ignored until she went to get a pilot, who ordered the game stopped immediately. At that point there was a mad scramble for the pot, and then everybody returned to his seat to be led in gospel hymns by Tyson's corner men for the balance of the eighteen-hour flight. I'm just kidding about that last part.

As I was heading to pick up my luggage at the airport, I found myself grasped from behind in a brief, but crushing, bear hug. I turned and saw the laughing face of Mike Tyson. "Mr. Mercante," he said in his curious, high-pitched lisp, "I want to tell you how proud I am that you refereed my fight. You know, Mr. Mercante, I'm a boxing historian, and I know all about you and the great fights you refereed. And, well, I'm just so proud you were there for me, also."

It was said with such boyish sweetness and such gentlemanly sincerity, it was hard to believe that this was the same vicious fighter I had been in the ring with just twenty-four hours earlier. I thanked Mike for his kind words and wished him good luck in the future.

Three months later, he pulverized a terrified Michael Spinks in a mere ninety-one seconds. The world seemed to be his for the taking, and Tyson seemed certain to dominate the heavyweight division well into the 1990s. Shockingly, his reign ended at the decade's dawn when James "Buster" Douglas knocked him out in the biggest upset in boxing history. Then came the rape conviction, and Tyson's life and career were in shambles.

I was deeply saddened to see a young man throw away such golden opportunities. Later, there was the bizarre ear-biting episode with Evander Holyfield, who so unexpectedly became the best heavyweight of his era. In 1988, when Tyson looked unbeatable, Holyfield was hardly more than a light heavyweight. But Holyfield had two things going for him: a tremendous fighting spirit and lion-hearted courage. What nature left out physically, modern training methods copiously supplied. Holyfield developed into a full-fledged heavyweight, something that would not have been possible just twenty or even fifteen years earlier.

As for Tyson, his last few years as a professional fighter have been unkind. Now approaching forty, Kid Dynamite is no kid and when he fights, which is infrequently, he loses more than he wins. His earnings of more than one hundred million dollars have vanished in the fog of reckless living. The young superstar champion, unbelievably rich and powerful with the whole world at his beck and call, ending up like an old, broken-down warhorse, impoverished and in debt, is an old story in boxing, as well as its saddest.

chapter 28

MARVELOUS MARV

I N THE 1980s and '90s, despite my age, I was refereeing more championship fights than ever. In fact, I was refereeing more fights than I did in the 1950s, the "Golden Era" of televised boxing. Since I wasn't getting any younger (indeed I had become old enough to collect Social Security), I made certain to maintain my rigorous exercise program that included jumping rope, chin-ups and push-ups. I tell young referees all the time to stay in shape, to make sure their muscles are firm and hard. A referee needs upper body strength to separate these big heavyweights. I remember George Foreman telling Gloria, "your husband is stronger than I am." That was laying it on pretty thick, of course; but the point is, I was a physical presence to deal with if a fighter, like Foreman, started in with the rough stuff.

In truth, refereeing fights was getting easier rather than harder for me. By the 1980s, I found that I had become a kind of elder statesman among referees. All the young fighters seemed to know who I was, the famous fights I had refereed and my reputation as a no-nonsense official. Some of them, to my discomfort, even asked for my autograph. The upshot was that, because of my reputation, I didn't have to earn the fighters' respect; in most cases I already had it. That is an important advantage that comes in handy in maintaining control of a fight.

The 1980s, to my surprise, even saw my broadcasting career re-ignite to a certain extent. Life in boxing was good, and I was enjoying the fruits of a successful career. But although the fight game was good to me, it was less kind to itself. Indeed, the general health of the sport was of mounting concern to me.

The mushrooming of champions became worse instead of better. Boxing had around seventy champions as opposed to the mere eight titleholders some thirty years ago. Worse yet, fighters were getting title shots with fewer than ten fights under their belts, and some of the referees and judges for these important fights were as inexperienced as the fighters. As a result, poor officiating and improper scoring became more and more of a problem. I was also very disturbed by ever increasing whispers about boxers using performance drugs to enhance their training as well as their physiques. If true, this was really alarming news. In the old days fighters didn't need drugs, they were energized by their own emotions.

As a result, I became very vocal about some of these abuses and advocated measures I thought could correct some of them, especially in the officiating area. Naturally, not everyone appreciated my candor, and I caught some flak for it. But that is exactly what I intended. I wanted to make people sit up and take notice. I've always believed in the Biblical injunction, "Physician, heal thyself." Healing itself was something boxing desperately needed to do.

While my outspokenness raised hackles on the backs of some necks, I'm glad to say, it didn't affect my refereeing assignments any. I continued to officiate top fights like Matthew Saad Muhammad–Dwight Muhammad Qawi, Alexis Arguello–Jim Watt, Ray Boom Boom Mancini–Jorge Morales, Marvin Hagler–Mustafa Hamsho, Hector Camacho–Edwin Rosario, and many others.

Of all these fighters, I had a special admiration for Marvelous Marvin Hagler, not only as a boxer but also as an individual. Like me, Hagler hailed from Brockton, Massachusetts, where, under the guidance of the Petronelli brothers, he cut a swath through the middleweight division. Hagler was a fighter's fighter, a workhorse, a war machine, totally committed to honing his craft. His unswerving commitment to conditioning, combined with his innate toughness and natural fighting ability, made this southpaw the best middleweight of his time. In truth, he was one of the finest 160-pounders to ever grace this storied division.

I know most boxing people will disagree with me, but I think, at his best, Hagler beats Carlos Monzon in a close decision. I might be wrong, but the "Mule," as Monzon was called, needed more room than Hagler would have given him. Great as he was, Monzon was just not as effective a fighter backing up. And I think Hagler would have backed him up. I saw Emile Griffith, past his physical prime and a division over his ideal fighting weight, give Monzon hell for fifteen rounds and nearly take his championship!

As tough as Marvin was, it wasn't all smooth sailing on his way to the top. He hit some roadblocks along the way and even after he got there. His first fight for the title ended in a draw with tough Vito Antuofermo. Vito had more guts than Evel Knievel and just fought his heart out. Although I thought Hagler did enough to win it, I had no argument with the decision. Marvin looked tight and uncertain throughout the fight, and Vito, whose chin should be enshrined at the Smithsonian, had made it close enough to convince the judges. It's a fact of life that champions always have the edge in that kind of situation.

But in a rematch Hagler stopped Antuofermo, and as champion, he was better than ever. The real articles usually are after they win the championship. They sweated blood to get the belt and are determined to keep it at any cost. The pride of a champion comes at birth, not with practice.

On October 19, 1984, I refereed Hagler's title defense against the Syrian boxer Mustafa Hamsho. The challenger was like an armadillo—you could hit him all night long and he would just stand there defiantly as if to ask if you had enough. He was that tough. Just as tough were the negotiations for the fight, which were all about gender. For the first time three female judges were to score the fight. Since the referee was no longer scoring fights, this meant that it would be just the ladies who would determine the winner of this bout. With the presidential election just two weeks away and Geraldine Ferraro running for vice president on the national ticket, it was boxing's version of keeping up with the times. The Hagler camp wanted nothing to do with it and complained loudly. Hagler never specified why this upset him so, but as the headliner on the Madison Square Garden card his objections carried the weight of his punches. The battle of sexes ended somewhat in a draw. There would be only one female judge, and the other two women judges would be assigned to the WBA junior middleweight title bout on the undercard.

Hagler would have no need of judges, female or otherwise, this night. Marvin made mincemeat out of Hamsho, cutting him to ribbons. It was all Hagler as he buzz sawed his way through Hamsho's limited defenses and battered him at will. All Hamsho could do was respond with a head butt, which I cautioned him strongly against. The butt attempt infuriated Hagler, who landed a solid right hook to the head that rocked Hamsho on his heels. As the challenger was falling backward the champion landed another solid right hand to the head, and the challenger sprawled onto the canvas.

Hamsho was up at the count of six, but Hagler was all over him. A right-left-right knocked Hamsho down again. They were all clean shots, and I was just about to stop it when Hamsho's manager, Al Certo, entered the ring, calling a halt to the hostilities. It was a mercifully short replay of their first encounter three years earlier as Hagler registered his fiftieth knockout while compiling a 60-2-2 record.

This fight set the table for Hagler's showdown the next year with the World Boxing Council's junior middleweight champion, Thomas Hearns. It would be one of the most memorable middleweight bouts of all time. Marvin stepped into the ring with Tommy Hearns and stepped out a boxing immortal. For sheer drama, ferocity and blood-lust in a compressed period of time, I only saw such a whirlwind of violence once before—when Rocky Graziano fought Tony Zale for the first time in a take-no-prisoners affair back in 1946. After nearly eight bloodcurdling minutes of punching, Hagler was still champ, and Hearns was carried half-unconscious from the ring. As famed sports writer Paul Gallico said about Jack Dempsey's four incredible minutes with Luis Firpo, "It was one sweet quarrel."

Hagler had conquered the world but not every mountain in it. Sugar Ray Leonard, of all people, was coming back to try to take his title. Marvin took the challenge personally. Where Hagler was a no-nonsense, get-the-job-done professional, Ray was a charmer, a wink-and-a-grin kind of guy—even the cadences of his fistic fury possessed a curious poetry. The media, in star-struck adoration, soaked it all up. Clearly, Hagler and Leonard were opposites that did not attract. In short, Hagler was dying to knock the glitz out of Sugar Ray.

They met on April 6, 1987, and after twelve interesting rounds, Leonard copped a split decision. It was the crowning moment in Ray's career and the absolute pits of Hagler's. He couldn't believe it. At first he was shocked, then appalled and finally embittered over the experience. Marvin was convinced he had won. He was angry with the judges, angry with the media that played up to Leonard's super-novaesque personality and angry with his managers for agreeing to a twelve-round bout when his superb conditioning better suited him for fifteen. Hagler would never fight again.

Some years later, I received an invitation from Hagler to be a guest at his wedding in Milan, Italy. Gloria and I got there a few days before-hand, and Marvin was the most gracious host imaginable. He told me about those trying days after the Leonard fight.

"I just had to get away, Arthur, far away. I drove to JFK Airport not knowing where I was going but just with an overwhelming feeling that I had to leave. I saw there was a flight to Milan, and I just caught it right there and then. It was a very impulsive thing to do, but fortunately everything worked out beautifully."

It sure did. Marvin liked everything about Italy—the people, the climate, the food. He decided to make a second home there and even got a few parts in some of those "Spaghetti Westerns" that nearly twenty years earlier had rocketed Clint Eastwood to stardom. Most importantly, he met a lovely Italian girl. They fell in love, and Gloria and I were delighted to personally wish them a lifetime of happiness together.

Whenever I go to Italy, I make it a point to look up Marvin. The last time, I invited Marvin and his wife to join us for dinner. He wouldn't hear of it and insisted we come to his place, instead, for a home-cooked gourmet meal. It was spectacular, and I mean the food and the company. Marvin has a beautiful home with a wonderful game room boasting a magnificent billiards table he is very proud of. In fact, the former Middleweight Champion of the World fancies himself quite a pool player.

People are always surprised that some of the nicest people they ever meet are fighters. It's so true—and Marvin Hagler is no exception. He's the golden rule.

chapter 29

IN MY FOOTSTEPS

R EFEREEING SO MANY fights was deeply gratifying, but the brightest spot of all was in 1984 when my son, Arthur Jr., made his debut as a professional boxing referee. As a father, I felt very proud to have my son follow in my footsteps. I was also, quite frankly, greatly relieved. Arthur's original plan was to become, like his revered Uncle Joe, a professional fighter, an idea that did not exactly move me to uncork a bottle of champagne in celebration.

While my love for boxing was as great as ever, I had, with time, become more sensitized to the suffering I saw in the ring. To see fighters my son's age absorb punishing blows bothered me in a way it never did when I was younger and the fighters were more my own age. So I tried to discourage Arthur by telling him that with so many other opportunities, why pick boxing? He remained unswayed, and the more I talked the more I heard the echo of my father's voice some forty-five years earlier telling me the exact same things.

Remembering my disappointment with my father's negative reaction to my own boxing plans, I decided that I wouldn't stand in Arthur's way provided he was willing to give it a one-hundred-percent effort.

It wasn't my son's ability I questioned (he did extremely well in the Golden Gloves), but rather his determination. To be honest, Arthur's training habits were not exactly Spartan-like. He could fight like hell for two rounds but then would start to putter out like a locomotive running out of steam. Frankly, his lack of endurance was hardly mystifying considering that roadwork was not part of his training regimen. Arthur just hated to get up early in the morning and run. Big mistake!

Don Dunphy told me that Rocky Marciano ran so many miles you would have thought he was in training for the Boston Marathon. Well, that's how it's done. As far as I'm concerned, you can't do too much roadwork. It strengthens a fighter's legs as well as vastly improving his wind. Believe me, a fighter whose legs go out on him is a dead duck— and I mean a dead duck! There is nothing more pathetic than to watch a talented fighter floundering in the ring, sucking wind, because he was too lazy to get up in the morning to do his laps.

Once it became clear that Arthur wasn't inclined to change his training regimen, I tried again to steer him in a different direction. "Arthur," I said, "you grew up in a nice, caring community; it's not exactly the kind of environment that breeds fighters. A fighter has to be hungry; he has to feel a sense of desperation about his circumstances. Your surroundings are just too comfortable to make the kind of sacrifices you need to make in order to be successful. Now look, I know how much you like boxing, and since you're physically strong and athletic, I think with the right experience you can make an outstanding referee."

That didn't interest him, so it was time to use my secret weapon. At a family gathering I took Uncle Joe aside and explained the situation. "So he wants to be a fighter," said the former boxer, thoughtfully rubbing his chin. "Leave it to me."

Inviting Arthur Jr. into the kitchen at our next family gathering, Uncle Joe sat him down and started giving him the facts of life. "You know, Arthur, boxing is a rough game," my uncle slowly began.

Arthur, like me, looked up to Uncle Joe. He had been a real, live, flesh-and-blood fighter, a man who had fought champions. "I know," Arthur said, "but you did it."

"Sure I did, Arthur, but at a terrible cost. Boxing can leave scars, you know. Terrible scars."

"Yeah, I know, but you're okay."

"Am I?"

"Yeah, you look great, Uncle Joe."

With that, in one sudden motion, Uncle Joe reached up to his right eye—his glass eye—and popped it out of the socket. Arthur sat there, too stunned to speak, just staring at a dark cavity where an eye should be. When the cavity began to tear up, Arthur couldn't bear to look anymore.

"You think I got this by playing pinochle? The fight game isn't all about glory, Arthur," said Uncle Joe very firmly. "It's cruel and hard. When I started fighting there was very little else I could do. Times were tough. But you—why, there is a whole world out there for you. Don't go through life half-blind like me, Arthur."

Uncle Joe's quite literally eye-popping performance was worth more than a thousand sermons from me. Arthur never knew his Uncle Joe— who never, ever, spoke about it—had lost an eye. The shock value was total. I think Arthur still bears the psychic scars.

Soon after, Arthur began to referee. At my insistence, he started out in the amateurs. After endlessly preaching about the need for referees to get more experience before they enter the professional ranks, I didn't want anyone saying I had lesser standards when it came to my own son. Arthur earned his stripes in the amateurs, and when he was properly seasoned he received his professional license.

I am proud to say that Arthur has made quite a name for himself in boxing, and he has done it all on his own merits. Technically, he is near perfect—although, as the old man, I reserve the right to gently admonish him from time to time. We have an understanding. I don't nitpick—that just demoralizes—but if I see something really improper, I do not to hesitate to bring it to his attention.

For instance, one night, while I was sitting at ringside to watch my son referee a fight, Arthur recognized one of the cornermen entering the ring with his fighter as an old friend. Instinctively, he walked over and embraced him. I nearly had a stroke. I'm an amiable guy. But when I'm in the ring to referee a fight, I'm downright unsociable. I don't want to have anything to do with the fighters and their entourages unless it pertains to the business at hand.

That night I took my son aside: "Look, Arthur, you are going to make a lot of friends in this business," I said, "but when you are on assignment you have no friendships with any of the principals involved in the fight. A referee, above all else, must maintain a posture of total impartiality and that extends to the cornermen. Suppose you had to penalize the other fighter, or, worse yet, disqualify him for some infraction? You would have left yourself wide open to charges of favoritism or worse."

Arthur sheepishly admitted he had used bad judgment and said he was sorry. "Don't be sorry, be smart," I told him. Arthur has been smart, and it has been deeply rewarding watching him grow as a referee. One of the biggest thrills of my life was when Arthur and I refereed the same night in the same ring. As far as anyone could remember, it was the first time a father and son refereed on the same card.

More than one boxing promoter has said to me, "You know Arthur, you used to be the best referee in the world, but now you are not even the best in your family." That always makes me feel good, not only because Arthur is my son but also because that's how I figure it should be. Things, after all, should get better.

Arthur had experienced the best of boxing. He had been heralded as a great young referee, a chip off the old block. It is intoxicating to hear these things said about yourself, to be in the thick of the action, to bask in the spotlight, to feel the excitement. Unfortunately, my son would soon enough find out that on the primrose path there are plenty of thorns amid the roses.

By its very nature, boxing is haunted by the specter of tragedy. While the fans love it, from the referee's perspective nothing is more terrifying than a knockout. How many times have I knelt over a stricken fighter, trying to coax him back to consciousness as nightmarish thoughts raced through my mind: *Does he have a brain concussion? Is he hemorrhaging? Is his skull fractured?* And worst of all: *Please God let him be alive.* These are the most horrific moments of all. Your heart is in your throat, you perspire rivers and you begin to feel a slow but sure panic building up inside of you. Believe me, it's the worst feeling in the world.

It is hard for someone who has never refereed to understand the intimacy of the ring. It is so small, so personal. In the heat of combat you can feel the fighters' sweat as you break the clinches, hear the sound of their heavy breathing as their lungs scream for oxygen. After a while, you even begin to feel the shock of the punches as if it were you on the receiving end. In a strange, psychological way you bond with the boxers, all three joined in a beautiful but fierce dance.

As the struggle progresses, the referee develops a feeling, especially when one of the fighters is hurt or bleeding or just vulnerable, that is unmistakably paternal. The desire to protect a fighter, to shelter him from injury, becomes paramount but is tempered by the nature of a sport that is so tied in with hurting and being hurt. As former Heavyweight Champion Ezzard Charles once told me, pain is part of this business. For the referee, achieving that delicate balance between limiting punishment and remaining faithful to a sport that demands it can become a source of unbearable tension.

I had a few very close calls through the years and the closest, as I mentioned before, happened during my very first Heavyweight Championship assignment: the Patterson–Johansson rematch in 1960. It was such a terrifying feeling to almost lose a fighter that the date— June 20, 1960, and *the exact time of the match—1:51—*is forever seared in my memory along with the image of the fallen Johansson, down for the count, blood trickling from his mouth, his right foot shaking with a grotesque tremor.

I was lucky—Johansson recovered to fight another day and thankfully I didn't experience the anguish again for another 42 years. And although I wasn't the referee (in fact I was safe at home, watching the bout on TV), the next time was much worse.

For this time it was my son Arthur Jr. playing the third man in. Like my near-miss event, Arthur's fight on the night of June 26, 2001, was a glitzy New York City affair on a June night outdoors. Set aboard the USS *Intrepid* Museum on the Hudson River, the fight—which some thought a mismatch from the start—ended in the worst possible outcome. Light heavyweight Beethavean Scottland was knocked out by his opponent, George Jones, in the tenth and final round. He was rushed from the ring by paramedics and after six days in a coma young Scottland perished from his injuries.

The boxing world was shaken and so was the Mercante family. The particulars of the fight are well known in boxing circles and don't need to be recounted by me. But I do want to talk a bit about how I viewed it both as a member of the professional boxing community and, more importantly, as a father.

I felt guilty. After all, it was because of me that my son had become a referee. I had taught him so much about the job: how to position yourself during a fight, how to maintain discipline and control of the bout, how to break a clinch, how to recognize danger signs, how to deal with unruly cornermen, and how to be in the scene but unseen. But I couldn't train or prepare him for a situation like this. Every fight and every fighter is different. Going into the ring, the referee typically knows little about the fighter's background, training, health and ability to take a punch.

I knew the risks, of course; I knew all about death in the ring. In 1953, the year before I started refereeing professionally, twenty-two fighters lost their lives, the most in boxing history. Me, I was lucky. I never had a fight that ended in a fatal injury. I had comforted other referees who had suffered tragedies in the ring, but never anyone so close to home, so close to my heart.

Arthur and I spoke several times a day. Boxing people called from all over to offer their support. Don't let anyone ever tell you boxing doesn't have a heart.

Referee Joe Cortez, an excellent official, told my son that the fighters know it is always a risk. "It happened to me," Joe said. "A fighter who left the ring under his own power collapsed in the dressing room shower and later died. It's a terrible thing, Artie; we do our best, but we are only human."

Arthur kept muttering he would never referee again. I told him I didn't want to hear that kind of talk. "You did nothing wrong, Arthur," I said. "Fighters have accidentally killed other fighters in the ring and have gone on to win championships. You must go on also." Arthur eventually did carry on, heeding the urging of his supporters and summoning his courage to work again. He has refereed many international championship bouts since.

The entire episode was the most heart-wrenching experience I ever had in decades of boxing. But I must say I'm proud of the compassion Arthur showed, proud of his humanity and his courage. To be deepened instead of destroyed by life's tragedies is the bravest thing any human being can do.

chapter 30

THE BOXING REF:
cool and collected

NEEDLESS TO SAY—but I'll say it anyway—refereeing is not an easy business. If you don't believe me just take a glance back at some of my predecessors and the current crop officiating today. A referee carries a great weight on his shoulders for he represents the conscience of the sport and gives it a semblance of civility. It is he who must enforce the rules and demonstrate its humane values. It is the referee's right to act mercifully, for boxing can be, and often is, pitiless.

Sometimes, however, it is the referee who must be pitied. I told the story about how Ruby Goldstein collapsed from heat exhaustion and had to be replaced when ringside temperatures soared to well over 100 degrees. Poor Ruby, an ex-fighter, never lived it down.

That steam bath, however, was virtually air-conditioned compared to the furnace George Siler worked in one night in 1899 at Coney Island. A full house came to watch Heavyweight Champion James J. Jeffries defend his crown against Tom Sharkey, a tough, tattooed, barrel-chested brawler who gave no quarter, nor asked for it. An enterprising promoter named William A. Brady was making the first attempt to film a fight under artificial lights, and the heat coming off the bulbs turned the ring into a sweat-soaked torture chamber.

In one of the great but almost forgotten contests in boxing history, the bout went the full twenty-five rounds with 400 arc lamps nearly cooking both the contestants and the referee. The fight was extremely close, and when George Siler raised that oak Jeffries called his right arm in victory, Siler was promptly smashed in the face with a red ripe tomato. The heat was so blistering, Jeffries would later blame it for his premature balding. Tom Sharkey went further. He claimed that Referee Siler was so delirious from the heat that he thought he was raising Sharkey's arm but, instead, raised Big Jeff's by mistake. When Siler heard, his only remark was "Tom's dreaming again."

Environmental conditions are one thing, of course, but they pale in comparison to the dangers a referee must face when confronting an angry crowd that believes him to be either blind, partisan or dishonest. I related my near brush with death by a crazed motorcycle gang in White Plains, but the baseball cry of "kill the ump" also applies to boxing referees and has probably been around as long as there have been referees. During the bare-knuckle days of 1860, the first international title bout took place between John C. Heenan of America and Tom Sayers of England. Partisans for Sayers became so threatening that, after the thirty-seventh round, the referee made himself scarce and high-tailed it out of town. The contestants fought the last five rounds without him!

And then there was Young Stribling, a handsome, charismatic and talented fighter, who not only possessed that good, old-fashioned Southern charm but also once held the all-time record for knockouts. When he wasn't riding his motorcycle, Stribling would often pilot himself from city to city for the privilege of knocking out the local hero.

Flying airplanes back in the '20s and early '30s was dangerous stuff, so Stribling really captured the public imagination and became the darling of fight fans everywhere. It was no surprise, then, when referee Harry Ertle declared Stribling's fight with Mike McTigue a draw right in Stribling's home state of Georgia, the verdict was greeted with something less than open-armed enthusiasm. An angry mob of infuriated partisans accosted Ertle and threatened to hang him from the nearest tree. Martyrdom not being in Ertle's immediate plans, he promptly reversed himself and awarded the fight to Stribling. Three hours later, when Ertle was safely out of Georgia, he telephoned the press services and the decision was again reversed.

Contrast this to the referee who officiated the fight between Light Heavyweight Champion Battling Siki, the Senegalese from West Africa, and the Irishman Mike McTigue. The African champion must have been one of the most naive fighters that ever lived. Incredibly, Siki agreed to defend his championship in Ireland against an Irishman on Saint Patrick's Day. The fight went the distance, but under those conditions no referee in his right mind was going to vote against a guy named McTigue. Siki left Dublin without the title.

Many years later, while watching the Jimmy Ellis–Floyd Patterson fight via satellite from Stockholm, Sweden, I—along with thousands of other television viewers—nearly choked on my beer and pretzel when referee Harold Valen awarded the fight to Jimmy Ellis. It was obvious to anyone with 20/200 vision that Floyd Patterson was the clear winner. Even though Floyd had demolished their hero, Ingo, the Swedes had taken Patterson to their hearts and the verdict for Jimmy Ellis (Valen had the sole vote) caused a virtual riot. The hapless Harold was lucky to get out alive.

Not that riots were unprecedented. Ex-champ Billy Conn, refereeing a fight in Mexico City, fled from the arena right to the airport after being chased by the largest army of Mexicans since Santa Anna laid siege to the Alamo. Conn never even bothered to stop at his hotel to pick up his luggage.

For those whose memories don't go back so far, let us not forget the riot that ensued after the Riddick Bowe–Andrew Golota bout when Golota was disqualified by the referee for repeatedly hitting below the belt. Not only the referee but also everyone in the Garden that night was in jeopardy as chairs and bottles went airborne in a frenzied melee.

No, the referee is not one of God's most loved creatures. So why would anyone want to be a referee? People become boxing referees, generally, because they love the sport and the excitement of the crowd, because they want to be part of the action. I'll tell you this: They certainly don't become referees because of the money. Believe me, it is not a profession you give up your day job for.

Most referees get paid only $200 to officiate a fight on the undercard and rarely does the pay exceed $800 for the big main event (which are few and far between) unless it is one of those super bouts. I remember when my colleague Jay Edson flew all the way to Japan to referee the bantamweight championship fight between Eder Jofre and Fighting Harada and was paid a measly $28.80—the lowest fee ever paid for a championship fight. On the other side of the spectrum, former Heavyweight Champion Jack Dempsey refereed the Ceferino Garcia–Glen Lee middleweight title bout back in 1939 and was paid a whopping $5,000. In the Depression year of 1939, you could buy a handsome house in the suburbs for $5,000.

But of course Dempsey was a fistic hero, a living legend. Olympian sums of that order were beyond the pale for us lesser mortals even though, and this is the God's honest truth, Dempsey was a lousy referee. So were most other champions. I don't know why people yearned for these champions to put on a bow tie and officiate, but you almost never saw it happen in other sports. Did you ever see Ted Williams or Willie Mays crouching behind the plate, calling balls and strikes?

But with fighters it was a different story. And as I said, they were generally a God-awful bunch. In the Ezzard Charles–Rex Layne bout, Dempsey scored almost every round even. In the second Ali–Liston fight, former Champion Jersey Joe Walcott was totally bewildered when Sonny went down, and he became engaged in a lively discussion with the timekeeper when Liston got up off the canvas and began again to trade punches with Ali. Joe Louis fared no better. In the second Joe Frazier–Jerry Quarry fight, the old Brown Bomber appeared frozen while a helpless Quarry was being pummeled. If Frazier had not let up and motioned for Louis to stop the fight, it could have ended tragically. I saw Rocky Marciano referee the Tom McNeely–George Logan fight in Boston Garden. Whenever the fighters got into close quarters (where Rocky did his best fighting), he would immediately break them up. All I can say is that Rocky the fighter would have hated Rocky the referee.

Celebrity refereeing is a bad idea; there is too much at stake just for the sake of ballyhooing a card by putting a former champion in to officiate. Early in the twentieth century things were different. In England referees would often remain outside the ropes to judge unless things really began to heat up. In the famed and infamous "Great White Hope" fight, when Jack Johnson defended his title against former Champion James J. Jeffries, promoter Tex Rickard invited President William Howard Taft to referee the fight. When the President of the United States declined, Rickard's next choice was Sir Arthur Conan Doyle, the author of the Sherlock Holmes stories, who also refused. Tex Rickard then decided to referee the fight himself. Can you imagine a promoter—Don King or Bob Arum—refereeing his own promotion? Unthinkable.

Fortunately, refereeing has become a much more serious business. What are the ingredients that make up a good referee? First, he must possess good judgment, a keen eye and quick reflexes. Temperamentally he must be cool and collected, not given to losing his composure in a crisis—after all, anything can happen in a fight. He must be in good physical condition and should have prepared himself for the pros by acquiring a wealth of experience in the amateur ranks. A good referee knows the rules and is not afraid to enforce them. He must know the signs of a serious brain injury such as glassy eyes, a weakened stance, arms hanging limp at the sides or an inability of the boxer to defend himself.

The timing of a contest's termination is crucial, and one cannot always rely on hard and fast rules. A referee must have the ability to think out of the box. I refereed one bout where the fighter showed none of the classic signs of a bad injury, yet every time he was hit solidly, he shivered momentarily as if an electric current had just coursed through his body. It frightened me. Though the fighter was neither down, wobbly nor glassy-eyed, I stopped the fight, triggering an automatic medical examination and brain scan.

A referee must be inconspicuous in the ring but always present when needed—he has to know how to break fighters and how to use forceful voice commands to maintain control and respect. Hand and arm signals must be crisp so that the fighters, managers, announcers and the audience will know what he is doing at all times. To be effective a referee must be in complete control of a bout and earn the respect of the fighters by being firm and fair. Finally, he must be neat in his attire and never wear jewelry, such as a wristwatch, rings, cuff links or a belt buckle. Jewelry like that can distract a fighter or, worse yet, cause injury when the referee is working at close quarters, such as when he's breaking a clinch.

If these facts are studied, practiced and conscientiously absorbed, then you too will have earned the right to be called "The Third Man in the Ring."

chapter 31

LIGHT AND HEAVY

Mexico is a beautiful country. It sits on a large central plateau flanked by the eastern and western coastal ranges of the Sierra Madre, which rises eight thousand feet near Mexico City. Some of the landscapes are breathtaking to behold: lush, scenic, exalting. This beauty, however, masks the backbreaking poverty that so many of its inhabitants labor under daily. Life has made Mexicans tough but never mean. I have come to truly love the country and the people who live there.

If I ever felt homesick while visiting Mexico, reading the newspapers there cured me. The front pages of all the major periodicals are filled with boxing news and color pictures of important matches, while the national and international news is all relegated to the back pages. I remember first traveling South of the Border with Nat Fleischer, founder of *The Ring* magazine and known all over the world as "Mr. Boxing." Fleischer was a grand little fellow, and the sport never had a better goodwill ambassador. On that maiden trip he took me all around, introducing me as "the best young referee in the world." To hear such lavish praise from Mr. Boxing himself made me swell with pride. It was also terribly exciting to be in a country that loved boxing so much. Even the Mexican national anthem, beginning with the words "Mexicans at the call of war!" reflects the country's indomitable fighting spirit.

The squared circle is a battleground of sorts, and Mexican boxers have, since time immemorial, been known as true warriors.

Collectively, they are the toughest group of hombres I ever encountered. There is something at the core of the Mexican fighter that just won't give up. In the fight game we call it heart.

Sometimes their boxing abilities don't match their great courage, but in the late 1980s there was one Mexican fighter I saw whose skills equaled his fighting spirit, at least before he became too sated with the good life to meet the terrible demands and sacrifices of this most grueling of sports.

His name was Julio Cesar Chavez, and in 1989 I refereed his bout with Alberto Cortes for the Lightweight Championship of the World. It was the first of many Chavez fights I did, although I had seen him in action before and was impressed with Chavez as a granite-chinned, savage body puncher who seemed unperturbed by anything the opposition threw at him. The Cortes fight confirmed my impression of Chavez as a fighter with the promise of greatness in him. Just watching him take Cortes apart and leave him for the sweepers was enough to convince anyone that this hombre was for real.

I didn't referee the famous Chavez–Meldrick Taylor fight, but it was a case study of Chavez's true effectiveness. A big controversy ensued when referee Richard Steele stopped the fight with just two seconds left and declared Chavez the winner by a TKO.

Many ringsiders and television viewers felt Taylor was ahead and was robbed of a sure victory by a last-second intervention. Nothing could be further from the truth. Though conscious, Taylor was a badly beaten fighter. Chavez's brutal body punches had taken a heavy toll, and after the fight Taylor had to be taken to the hospital where the doctor examining him said the fighter was so banged up it looked like he was in a car wreck.

That's what a canny body puncher can do to you. Body punches are not concussive, nor do they open cuts; but their effect is nevertheless deadly. "Kill the body and the head will die," is an adage as old as boxing itself. Chavez was the best body puncher in the business.

Since I refereed fights involving Chavez as well as some of Roberto Duran's bouts, I'm often asked who would have won if they had met in their respective primes. That's a tough call. Clearly they were the two best lightweights of the last forty years or more, although you would have to put Carlos Ortiz right up there with them. If forced to pick, I'll pick Duran by decision in a pier-sixer I'd want a ringside seat for if I weren't lucky enough to be the third man in the ring.

I still don't know what the "Continental Featherweight Championship" is, but I do know that the fight that decided it in 1992 was one of the most memorable ones I refereed that decade. Kevin Kelley and Troy Dorsey were the contestants. Dorsey was a kickboxing champion turned boxer. Very few kickboxers have successfully made the transition to boxing, mostly because their punching abilities are severely limited. Dorsey was no exception; he might have been able to kick, but he couldn't punch a lick. What Dorsey had going for him was his remarkable physical condition, which allowed him to fight full speed ahead for every second of every round.

From the opening bell Dorsey was on the more-skilled Kelley like a cheap suit, giving him no breathing room. It was punch, punch and then punch some more. Fortunately for Kelley, Dorsey's punches pestered rather than pulverized. But while Dorsey's blows could not seriously hurt Kelley, the sheer volume of them was simply staggering.

I have been told the Kelley–Dorsey fight still holds the "Punch Stat" record for the greatest number of punches thrown in a twelve-round fight. While never a "Punch Stat" fan (to me it was just another gimmick), the Kelley–Dorsey stats give some indication of the incredible pace of the fight. Ultimately, Kelley's superior skills prevailed, and he won a close decision—but what a hurricane of a brawl!

The light heavyweight division has always been "the sick man of boxing." The division is composed of fighters too big for the storied middleweight division and too small to compete in the big-moneyed heavyweight division. Light heavyweights are cursed to wander in "no-man's-land" between boxing's two glamour divisions.

Nevertheless, I've seen some great light heavies whose skills were comparable to any fighter's, regardless of division. Billy Conn, who made an immortal effort to wrest the heavyweight title from Joe Louis, was certainly one; Archie Moore, a great virtuoso of the Sweet Science, was another and one of the most colorful fighters ever; and of course dynamite-punching Bob Foster, who owned the light heavyweights when he was champ, stands out as well. Perhaps the best of them was Ezzard Charles, who defeated Archie Moore three out of three before he moved up in class to win the coveted heavyweight crown. Mostly, however, the excitement level among fight fans for the light heavy-weights was considered to be right up there with PBS fund-raising telethons. But in the last decade of the century one fighter would change that impression.

In the '90s, the man at the top of most people's "pound for pound" list was Roy Jones Jr., Light Heavyweight Champion of the World. I refereed several of Jones's fights and even rang in the new millennium by refereeing his fight with David Telesco at Radio City Music Hall on January 15, 2000. My God—the years just flew!

It was the first time a fight was ever held at that historic theatre, which had just undergone extensive renovations. As impressive as the theatre was, the setup was not very conducive for a boxing match. The ring was situated too far from the spectators, who practically needed binoculars to see the action. For all of Radio City's palatial opulence, I'll take the cramped, musty, pedestrian architecture of Saint Nick's Arena any day of the week.

The fight itself was mostly non-eventful, with Jones winning a rela-tively easy decision. There was no denying Roy's gifts as a fighter. Yet for all the excitement he created and all the praise that was heaped upon him, I am still not convinced of his fistic greatness. There seemed to be something missing, that extra something that separates the greats from us mere mortals. Perhaps I sensed he was a bit gun-shy or it could have been his absence of a classical style or the lack of real competition in his division. Or, maybe, it was just something else I can't put my finger on.

But while Jones may be damned lucky that Bobby Foster fought in a different era, he still stood head and shoulders above any other light heavyweight in the world. More importantly, whenever he fought there was a palpable energy that roused the crowd to high-pitched excitement. Jones generated renewed interest in the game, and for that boxing owes him a debt of gratitude.

Like a breath of fresh air, when boxing gets a fighter like Roy Jones Jr. and fights like Oscar De La Hoya–Shane Mosley and Felix Trinidad–Fernando Vargas, it shows that even with its weakened pulse and fainter heartbeat, the sport is going to be around for a long time to come.

As the twentieth century finally wound down, I realized my career was also coming to a close. While I still refereed fights featuring such champions as Lennox Lewis and Roy Jones, I could see that this large chapter of my life was almost written. This never hit home more than the night I refereed the heavyweight championship bout between Riddick Bowe and Buster Mathis Jr. Nearly 30 years earlier, I had refereed a fight with Mathis's father, Buster Senior, when he fought Joe Frazier.

When Jersey Joe Walcott knocked out Harold Johnson back in 1950, the boxing fraternity roared over the fact that old Jersey Joe had knocked out Johnson's father, Phil Johnson, a decade and a half earlier. I chuckled about it like everyone else. But now it occurred to me that, like old Jersey Joe, my career had spanned generations, and I came to realize more than ever before that, for each of us, the world truly is round.

It is also crooked. The controversy that swirled around the Bowe–Mathis Jr. affair was nothing to chuckle about. It gave me a taste of what might have happened in Tokyo if Mike Tyson had hit Tony Tubbs while he was sitting on the canvas and I thus had to disqualify him. Same situation—only this time it was Buster Mathis on the canvas with Bowe taking a pot shot. Only Riddick didn't miss.

I never thought this match should have been made in the first place. Young Buster had some of his father's elusiveness, and though he inherited his father's prominent tendency toward corpulence, he was nowhere near Buster Sr.'s height or massiveness, nor could he move around the ring with the quickness and agility of his old man. But whereas Mathis Jr. was not a born fighter, the boxing fairies had liberally sprinkled their charms on baby Bowe. He was endowed with imposing physical dimensions, power in both hands and a sizable amount of natural boxing talent. Unfortunately, Riddick was basically lazy and indifferent about his chosen profession and despite winning two heavyweight titles he never reached his full potential.

This was Bowe's first fight since he had lost the WBA and IBF belts to Evander Holyfield, nine months earlier. Holyfield, in turn, lost to Michael Moorer, but there was no interest in a Bowe–Moorer match. Lennox Lewis, the WBC heavyweight champion, was a more attractive and lucrative fight. There was no love lost between Bowe and Lewis, and since both were big and talented the match was a natural. That Lennox Lewis was from Britain also flavored the match with a trans-Atlantic rivalry. But first, Bowe would have to get by Mathis, who hardly seemed insuperable since Buster's two-fisted attack had all the cumulative, concussive power of an animated pillow fight.

Both fighters came into the ring overweight. Clearly, this wasn't going to be a replay of the "Thrilla in Manila," and fight fans sniffed it out for a stinker. The Atlantic City Convention Center Ballroom, which seats only 3,000, was still half-empty at the opening bell.

The fight was all Bowe—too big, too strong for brave-but-blubbery Buster Jr. The younger Mathis, though, was a good ducker and not easy to hit solidly. So while Bowe scored with some telling blows, many of his punches sailed harmlessly overhead. Late in the fourth round, Mathis was tagged, and he willingly sunk to one knee to collect himself. Instead of going to a neutral corner, Bowe very purposefully hauled off and clobbered him. It was a blatant infraction of the rules, and I was on the precipice of disqualifying the former champion when Larry Hazzard, New Jersey State Athletic Board commissioner, intervened and ruled the fight a no-contest. Hazzard's action, virtually unprecedented, spared Bowe from suffering a second straight loss and maybe losing a mega-bonanza match-up with champion Lennox Lewis.

I was absolutely opposed to a no-contest ruling and was very direct in stating my objections to Hazzard and my intention to award the fight to Mathis on a foul. After consulting with his deputies, the commissioner overruled me. Larry informed me I couldn't disqualify Bowe because he had won every round. "We'll call it a no-contest," Hazzard stated with a tone of finality.

I thought Larry was dead wrong. True, the big heavyweight was pitching a shutout, but that didn't grant him immunity from disqualification. As the fight progressed, Bowe was growing increasingly frustrated by Mathis's elusive tactics and his inability to land the coup de grace. With Mathis on the canvas, the former champ just lost his head and unloaded a haymaker at the inviting target. It was a vicious punch that could have been lethal to the helpless and stricken Mathis. There was absolutely no doubt the punch was premeditated and intentional, and it should have earned Bowe a disqualification.

Although Riddick apologized effusively to me in the immediate aftermath (he should have been apologizing to Buster), the damage was done. I refused to endorse Hazzard's decision. The next day the sports section's headlines trumpeted: "Mercante Stands by Decision."

Eleven years later, I still stand by it. Bowe should have been disqualified . . . period!

Hazzard said very little to me after that, but then, he had said so little before. The sports writers and boxing people, in general, praised my steadfastness.

Bruce Kielty, the matchmaker for the fight, weighed in on my side. "There isn't one person in boxing who can question the integrity of Arthur Mercante," he said, "but what the New Jersey commission did by ruling it a no-contest is a national disgrace."

Sports journalist Anthony Carter Paige wrote, "If there has been one constant in boxing, besides slime, corruption and greed, it has been the steady professionalism of Arthur Mercante."

I didn't merit all this praise. As far as I was concerned I was just doing my job. It was, however, nice to know that the standards I held for myself and my profession did not go unappreciated. Larry Hazzard's cold silence is a small price to pay for that.

chapter 32
THE MORE THINGS CHANGE . . .

THERE IS AN old saying that the more things change, the more they stay the same. In my time boxing has undergone many changes and facelifts. Some have been good for the sport; others have been less than desirable. Since my involvement in boxing has been life-long, I'm probably in as good a position as anyone to evaluate some of these changes.

Let us begin with the boxer's stock and trade—the gloves. Today's gloves are more heavily padded and better engineered for punching than before. I like that because they are less likely to cause facial cuts, which often result in a premature stoppage of a contest. It is heartbreaking to stop a fight—especially a competitive one—because of a cut. The fewer cuts, the better.

Another change for the better is that the laces of the gloves are wrapped in tape, making them unavailable to be used as a weapon to inflict eye injuries. Today the use of duct tape on the gloves has greatly reduced the infliction of the type of eye injuries that used to be epidemic in boxing. On the other hand, duct tape has a tendency to unwrap, which interrupts the action.

After some serious soul-searching, I have come to support the reduction of championship fights from fifteen rounds to twelve rounds that followed the tragic Ray Mancini–Duk Koo Kim lightweight title fight in 1982. Kim died several days after the fight. As a strong traditionalist, I did not find this an easy decision to make. I am well aware that some of boxing's most memorable moments have occurred late in scheduled fifteen-rounders: Joe Louis's comeback KO over Billy Conn and Rocky Marciano's KO of Jersey Joe Walcott made thirteen a lucky number for both of them.

There are countless other examples, including Frazier downing Ali with that big left hook in the fifteenth round of their first fight, and Sugar Ray Leonard coming from behind to stop Thomas "Hit Man" Hearns in the fourteenth round of their classic match-up. These dramatic endings were only possible because fights were scheduled for fifteen rounds.

But I also remember the needless carnage of some of those longer fights: a battered but proud Jake LaMotta refusing to fall as Sugar Ray Robinson beat him to a pulp in the thirteenth round of a fight so brutal it became forever known as the "St. Valentine's Day Massacre"; Muhammad Ali and Joe Frazier savaging each other in Manila to the point that both ended up shells of their former selves. I also have disturbing memories of the first Alexis Arguello–Aaron Pryor fight, and of Larry Holmes using Randall "Tex" Cobb as a human punching bag for fifteen rounds. It was actually the Holmes–Cobb fight, right on the heels of Mancini–Kim, that precipitated the change to twelve rounds.

Holmes couldn't miss Cobb if he was blindfolded, but Tex, with a chin seemingly on loan from Plymouth Rock, refused to turn out the lights. He suffered a terrible one-sided thrashing on network television. Howard Cosell, announcing the fight, became so disgusted that he vowed never again to broadcast a professional fight. (Later, the ever-sardonic Cobb proclaimed that driving Cosell from the microphone was a gift to humanity that he could only surpass if he discovered a cure for cancer.)

When I came out in favor of twelve-round championship fights, you would have thought I had endorsed polygamy, communism and the making of graven images. Some of my oldest and dearest friends in boxing accused me of growing soft. Well, there are worse things—even in boxing. Others argue that fifteen rounds is the true championship distance, separating the men from the boys. Maybe—but this is not enough to outweigh the safety reasons that more than justify the twelve-round limitation.

Boxing has also made enormous strides in protecting a stricken fighter. The first such measure was the neutral corner rule, which requires a fighter scoring a knockdown to go to the farthest neutral corner while the referee tolls the count of ten. More changes came, albeit slowly. In 1953, the NYSAC adopted the compulsory eight-count rule in all fights except championship ones. Ten years later, the eight-count rule became mandatory in all title fights.

While I wholeheartedly back the use of the compulsory count in all boxing matches, I have no use for the latest innovation. Frankly, I despise the standing eight-count. It does nothing but take the referee off the hook—no pun intended. More often than not, standing eight-counts prolong fights that should be stopped. If a fighter is too hurt to continue or cannot defend himself, the bout should be stopped, not delayed. Too many times, I witnessed this only helping the fighter dishing out the punishment, not the one taking it.

There was a time when boxing referees were more like spectators than officials. While things have improved, I would like to see referees become still more active when it comes to protecting a fighter. Of course officiating can be overdone, but when it is not done enough the results can be tragic.

Boxing deserves a lot of credit for taking the training of referees seriously, and while much still needs to be done, I am as proud of my efforts in this regard as I am of anything else in my career. I conduct seminars for referees throughout the world, teaching the finer points of officiating, and also how to recognize dangerous situations, when to stop a fight and how best to protect the fighter from serious injury.

Another outstanding reform requires a downed fighter to rise under his own power when the bell rings, ending the round. Too often, seconds have dragged an unconscious fighter back to his corner and then pushed him off his stool for the next round. A vintage example of this occurred in the Muhammad Ali–Cleveland Williams fight. At the end of the second round, Williams was flat on his back, his arms stretched over his head like rabbit ears on an old television set. Hauled back to his corner, the half-conscious Williams was shoved out for the third round for further pummeling until Referee Harry Kessler mercifully intervened.

When the WBA suggested a rule change that would take the privilege of scoring a fight away from the referee on the grounds that keeping score and minding the fighters put too much on the referee's plate, I was one of only two referees at the Las Vegas World Boxing Convention to vote against it. I always felt that the referee is in the best position to see the blows landed and gauge their effectiveness. I appealed to my dear friend José Sulaiman, president of the WBC, voicing my great disappointment (perhaps I was a bit overwrought when I said I felt the measure was emasculating) over this decision. He was sympathetic and soothing and told me that not every referee is Arthur Mercante. Since I have known José for years and have great respect for his opinion, I relented.

Although I miss scoring a fight (especially feeling as I did that my scores were usually on the mark), I do now see the point of leaving that burden out of the referee's hands. I understand the anxieties a referee feels without having the additional worry of scoring a fight. Today's boxing referees have far more responsibilities and pressures to deal with than ever before. If taking them out of the voting bloc alleviates some of the burden, then I am for it.

The way a fight is scored has been markedly improved. The round system is an antiquated way of scoring a fight and is as likely as not to result in a disputed decision. If a fighter knocks his opponent down, that should mean more in the scoring than when his opponent out-jabs him in another round. As I mentioned elsewhere, the first Ali–Frazier fight was very close in terms of rounds, but less so under the point system. On my card, Frazier would have won the eleventh and the fifteenth rounds by two-point margins, but under the round system Frazier's margin of victory was, in effect, treated as a one-point difference.

A weighted scoring system is the best calibrating system devised, but it should be based on a four-point-must system rather than a ten-point-must system. No fighter wins a round 10–0. Any round in which one fighter has more than a four-point advantage is a fight that has no business continuing and should be stopped.

Another wonderful recent development has been the ever-growing sophistication of pre-fight medical testing, which among other things measures brain damage. Add to this the requirement of ringside paramedics, the compulsory suspension period after a boxer is knocked out and the drug tests taken before and after a fight, and it makes the case that boxing has the capacity to govern itself. The idea that a Federal Boxing Commission is needed to bring order to the sport is sadly mistaken. The last thing boxing needs is Washington bureaucrats running it. It would be a case of the cure being worse than the disease.

The sport needs to follow the path of the Association of Boxing Commissioners, which has worked hard to institute uniformity and standardization of the rules, and require that bouts be sanctioned by state authorities. The commissioners should also require promoters to provide health insurance for the guys taking the punches. Some of these reforms are long overdue, but the important thing is that they are being done and they are paying dividends in terms of a fighter's health and well-being.

Though boxing has achieved notable victories along these fronts, it has somewhat regressed in other areas. One dubious development has been the multiplication of so many fringe sanctioning bodies, each jealously claiming its own champion. To make matters worse, at present there are about seventeen weight classes. Not even Peggy Cass could keep track of our current titleholders.

The upshot is a meteoric rise of second-rate fighters becoming title contenders, gross mismatches and fighters becoming champion after only fifteen fights or less. Moreover, with so many champions there is no incentive to have the best fighters meet. Better they should be champion of some new organization than risk it all against an opponent of comparable talent. Gone are the days when Jimmy McLarnin and Barney Ross, the two best welterweights of the 1930s, fought for the title *three times* in a span of twelve months! Today, fans are often cheated out of seeing the better matches because of the politics of the alphabet groups.

Another sea change has nothing to do with the rules of boxing but rather with the athletic culture of America itself. For the first thirty-five years or so of my life, boxing was second only to baseball in public popularity. When I was growing up, boxing gyms and fight clubs were everywhere. Kids were always putting on the gloves and sparring, not only in gyms but also in backyards, schoolyards and just about anywhere they could find an open space. Boxing was as big then as the martial arts are today with the kids.

After World War II, America's newfound prosperity, combined with televisions in the home, translated into a disappearance of boxing gyms and local fight clubs. Gone were the neighborhood and ethnic rivalries that generated so much interest and excitement. Of course you could catch the fights on television all the time. Television heroes replaced neighborhood ones. And by the mid-1950s, team sports such as football and basketball began to take the sporting public by storm and, except for the real big fights, America's love affair with boxing cooled off.

I often find myself longing for the days when the great championship fights were held in Madison Square Garden, the Polo Grounds, Yankee Stadium and Ebbets Field. There was something about the atmosphere and venue of those locales that gave the fights an aura of grandeur that today's gambling casinos just can't match. Even more disturbing is the professional-wrestling, carnival-like aspect that has started to attach itself to some of boxing's important matches. Jorge Paez dressing as a nun, Angel Manfredi in a devil's mask, and the antics of other boxers have made a mockery of the sport.

It's time to move away from this nonsense. Leave the costumes and the histrionics to the phony pro-wrestlers. Boxing is not choreography or theatrical entertainment—it's a sport. Muhammad Ali was funny and entertaining reciting his pugilistic poetry and making bold predictions, but for all his showmanship he was never a clown when he walked into the ring.

Another marked difference between today and years gone by is the way boxers train. Since the days of John L. Sullivan and even before, boxing was all bag punching, roadwork, jumping rope, sparring and floor calisthenics. Today, high-tech weight training has been added into the equation. For decades weightlifting was believed to be taboo in boxing. Lifting weights made a fighter muscle bound, according to the conventional wisdom, depriving him of flexibility.

When Muhammad Ali saw the scene in *Rocky* where Sylvester Stallone was lifting weights to prepare for his fight with Apollo Creed, Ali turned to his companions, shook his head and called it "the worst thing a fighter could do." I thought so, too, and so did every boxing trainer I ever knew.

But how things have changed in the last twenty-five years or so! Weight training has become a religion with top boxers, especially heavyweights. Almost all are now involved in some kind of strength program. While I have not been completely converted, there is no question that weight training has developed into a science and has revolutionized the physique of the modern athlete. The muscularity of some of these fighters is truly astonishing and wholly unprecedented. Call it the "Godzilla Complex" if you will, but while I think it is overdone, the new commandment of boxing is that size does matter, and some boxers are willing to do anything to get it.

Evander Holyfield is probably the poster child for the new physique in boxing. Without the iron, I doubt if Holyfield would have been more than a conditioned 190 pounds. I am equally convinced that George Foreman's longevity, like that of so many other athletes, is a result of some serious weight training.

Unfortunately, this zeal to get bigger and stronger has led some past the weight room and into the laboratory. Steroids combined with the use of weights can increase muscle mass dramatically and also help restore fatigued muscles quickly so that an athlete can engage in more strenuous workouts. Anabolic steroids and weightlifting go together like bread and butter. But it is not a marriage made in heaven. Recent surveys have estimated that nearly a million teenage boys are already using steroids. I find this very disturbing, not only because it can be harmful but also because there is something philosophically incompatible about mixing performance-enhancing drugs and sports. Athletic achievement should be about character, not chemistry. It is, after all, the athletes we elect to the Hall of Fame, not their pharmacologists. While I know that steroid testing is expensive and airtight detection difficult, steroid use is cheating, and boxing should follow the example of the International Olympic Committee and do everything in its power to make sure that everyone is competing on a level playing field.

I always thought I was ahead of my time in supporting women's athletics. Ever since I was a young man, I have encouraged women to become more involved with sports, and I have always felt that athletic competition holds the same benefits for them as for men. Today you see women performing with great skill on basketball courts and on soccer and lacrosse fields, as well as at track-and-field events. It is wonderful, and there is no bigger fan of these women athletes than I.

However, today we also have the phenomenon of women boxing. I have come to know many of these women as both athletes and people. They are great competitors and wonderful individuals, and some have exhibited real skill and dedication in their craft. Knowing many of them and feeling the kindness and respect they have so generously shown me has meant the world to me. Nevertheless, I cannot countenance the idea of female boxers and have made my point by declining countless opportunities to referee women's bouts. My instinct has always been to protect women, never to stand by and see them hurt. I will continue to champion the right of women to be in the corporate world, in the corridors of government and on the athletic fields, but the idea of women fighting in the ring is as offensive as that of women fighting in the trenches of war.

chapter 33
STEPPING INTO THE HALL

E ARLY IN 1995, I was notified of my selection for the International Boxing Hall of Fame in Canastota, New York. Hall of Fame Director Ed Brophy said since I had reached the pinnacle of my career and contributed so much to boxing as a referee, I was an obvious choice of the selection panel. Obvious or not, I was deeply honored to be chosen by my peers.

There were so many things I felt grateful for, not the least that at age seventy-five I was in good health and in command of all my faculties, but to be honored by the sport I love was truly humbling, especially as a member of an induction class that included such luminaries as my boyhood idol, Max Baer; trainer of champions Cus D'Amato; and the fabulous (but almost forgotten) 1940s Lightweight Champion Bob Montgomery. Bob's classic four-fight series with Beau Jack ranks as one of the most thrilling in the division's history. For their August 1944 fight, fans bought war bonds in lieu of tickets. When you look at Montgomery, Beau Jack, Joe Louis and others, it makes you feel mighty proud of what some of these fighters sacrificed for their country. They are truly Boxing's Best!

Pleased and excited as I was about my induction, Gloria and the boys were even more so. Gloria decided to make the four-day induction weekend in June a real family festival and began calling all our relatives, including those still living in Brockton, Massachusetts. When we arrived in Canastota, it was like a reunion of the Mercante family.

Some of these relations I hadn't seen in twenty-five, or even thirty years. It was such a warm and wonderful feeling, reestablishing family ties that had unfortunately faded away with time and distance. Once reunited, however, the warmth and affection was as strong as it had ever been.

Just as gratifying was the attention I received from the fans and the boxing fraternity. I was greeted everywhere with handshakes and pats on the back, as well as showered with expressions of congratulations. A host of superlatives were spoken about my refereeing career and about me personally. Their praise was much too generous, though I made it a point to accept each compliment, no matter how extravagant, as graciously as I could.

At the "Banquet of Champions" dinner at the Rusty Rail Party House, Joe Frazier bulled his way through the overflow crowd, much like he bowled over opponents in the ring, and gave me a huge bear hug. Joe looked great—like he could still smoke for fifteen rounds. Then from halfway across the room, I caught the eye of my dear friend, former Champion Carmen Basilio, who raised his glass to me. What a class guy—what a great fighter. Canastota was his hometown; the people who lived here loved him. And why not?—Basilio was one of those fighters who embodied the true guts of boxing. One of only two fighters who ever knocked down the great Kid Gavilan, Basilio's classic fights with Tony DeMarco and Sugar Ray Robinson were studies in determination and raw courage and will be remembered as long as the sport itself.

Hall of Famer Willie Pep also came over to shake hands. Pep was a boxing genius. Trying to hit Willie, it was said, was like trying to stamp out a grass fire. Willie, a great favorite, was peppered with questions by the fans.

"Hey, Willie," yelled one fan, "what was your toughest fight?"

"My third wife," Willie shot back. "She was half Irish, half Puerto Rican and could fight like hell."

The people roared—proving Willie's verbal timing was as swift and accurate as his counterpunching.

The man I call the Ph.D. of the Sweet Science, "Professor Archie Moore," greeted me not with the conventional handshake but by bumping fists with me. Archie once explained he doesn't shake hands ever since he noticed so many people leaving restrooms without washing. "Its disgusting," Archie told me. He had a point, and in fact I was a bug on personal cleanliness myself. One day while in a restroom of a five-star hotel in Manhattan, I saw a well-dressed man walk out without washing his hands. Normally, I would just shake my head at such a breach of hygienic decorum, but, feeling indignant, I followed him out and berated him for his unsanitary habits. Mortified, he apologized and sheepishly went back into the restroom to wash up.

Then it was time for our dinner orders. There didn't seem to be enough chairs and tables to accommodate everyone. The Mercantes alone took up several tables. Somehow the staff at Rusty Rail came through, and soon everyone was seated.

I was touched to see so many family members and colleagues there for the greatest professional honor of my lifetime—some just in spirit: Mom and Pop were no longer with us, and my uncles Joe and Neib, who had such a powerful and beneficial influence in my formative years, were also gone. I felt a pang of sadness at their absence but consoled myself with the thought that they were remembered with love and gratitude, and that was what really mattered.

My beautiful and wonderful wife, Gloria, glowed softly at my side. No matter how much I could say in tribute to Gloria, it will never be enough. Without her, my career, the wonderful life that I led, would not have been possible. As a wife, a mother, a lifelong companion, she is the greatest champion I ever knew.

My four boys now grown into manhood were there with their wives. I am so proud of all of them. Glenn, my oldest, is in the entertainment business; Jim is an Admiralty Lawyer and holds the rank of captain in the United States Naval Reserve; Arthur, a stagehand foreman, works at the Metropolitan Opera House and, of course, is following the old man's footsteps in the ring; and Tom, my youngest, is a chiropractor.

The program started. Now and then someone came up for an autograph, others maintained a respectful distance as we were served dinner. Bob Foster, the former great light heavyweight champ, was speaking at the dais, recalling his fight with Joe Frazier back in 1970. He was quite a raconteur, and he had the crowd laughing uproariously—none louder, however, than Frazier himself, who seemed on the verge of splitting a gut.

I began to thumb through an old brochure someone handed me on the first Patterson–Johansson fight. That was thirty-five years earlier, which didn't seem possible.

Time has a way of playing tricks like that. As I reminisced, I realized it was more than seventy years ago that a kid in short pants with a funny looking haircut stood in a cornfield in Brockton, Massachusetts, watching men he saw as gods pound the bags, skip the ropes and spar in a makeshift ring—taking in sights, sounds and smells that would sear a lifelong love in his heart for this cruel but noble sport. And now the man who had been that boy was about to be inducted into the International Boxing Hall of Fame. It all seemed too incredible to have happened.

My reverie was broken when the emcee invited my son Jim to the dais to say a few words. That wasn't on the official program, and as Jim walked to the podium I wondered what was up. At the mike, Jim looked very calm and composed, and said he had a few words to say about tonight's inductee Arthur Mercante. The noisy room quieted, and I could feel Gloria affectionately squeeze my hand.

Jim began on a light note, telling the audience that growing up in the Mercante household was like living in boot camp. Every morning, the Mercante boys had to crank out ten chin-ups before breakfast, ten more before dinner and another ten at bedtime. "'Sound mind, sound body,' was my father's motto," Jim noted.

"There has been a lot said on what a great boxing referee Arthur Mercante is," Jim continued. "Well, he certainly is that. What hasn't been said is what a wonderful father and great role model he has been for all of us."

Then my son read a poem he wrote in honor of the occasion. Its title was "Ode to a Ref."

The third man in the ring,
As he is often referred,
Is "the man in charge" of the bout—
His authority not to be deferred.
The instructions are given before the sound of the bell:
Obey the rules, or there'll be hell.
"Let's have a clean fight" is the referee's cry.
The authoritative figure in fitted shirt and bow tie.
Only three commands, "Stop," "Box," and "Break,"
Are his stock in trade
But it takes much more than this to make the grade.
Knowing when to stop the fight is key,
Compassion for the fighters, and fitness are three.
In the scene, but unseen, is also a good start;
For the few who have mastered this, it sets them apart.
And earning respect while preventing the foul
Will halt the trainer from tossing in the towel.
His is not the knockout or decision,
His is to control the fight with precision.
It used to be the ref would score;
Unfortunately, that exists no more.
After the fight the ref gets no prize;

But sometimes he will be recognized by a fight fan's eyes.
Not many will be known as "illustrious" or as "legend,"
And while few make it to the top of their game,
Fewer still rate high enough
To be inducted in the Boxing Hall of Fame.
For there is no greater achievement,
No greater tribute, or fame,
Than for your peers to enshrine, forever, your name.

I was still reeling from Jim's tribute when I was told that Arthur Jr. would be the key speaker to introduce me at the International Boxing Hall of Fame ceremonies for the formal induction the very next morning.

It was thrilling news, and I couldn't have been more delighted. Of all my sons he was the logical choice to introduce me because he had become, and still is, my successor as a boxing referee. Don Ackerman, the president of the Hall of Fame, introduced Arthur Jr. as a well-respected member of the boxing community. I stood at Arthur's side during his wonderful speech and presentation. I shed a few tears at his touching words about the old man.

Arthur then presented me with a beautiful clay rendering of Ali, Frazier and me during the championship fight. It now sits in a cherished spot in my living room. "Ali–Frazier I" has become the signature moment of my career, and I couldn't have received a more appropriate gift symbolizing my life in the ring and in some ways my own life as well. In a sense everyone's life is one big fight. There are some rounds we win and some we lose. Sometimes we find ourselves knocked on the seat of our pants, but the important thing is to get up and keep punching. Just like Ali and Joe, no matter how tough things get, we need to be ready to go the distance.

EPILOGUE

A LL GOOD THINGS must come to an end. I made up my mind that 2001 would be my last year refereeing. It was a difficult decision, but it was time. I was eighty-one years old, and even though I felt good, I knew I could not go on forever. I remember Larry Holmes once telling me that the mind makes appointments the body can't keep. What's true for an old fighter also holds true for referees. I certainly didn't want to end up embarrassing myself, and so I decided to leave while I was still on top of my game.

I wanted to go out in a championship fight. It would be, I thought, a fitting valedictory. When I heard that I would do the middleweight title bout between Bernard Hopkins and Felix Trinidad at Madison Square Garden on September 29, 2001, I couldn't have been more pleased.

First, however, the NYSAC asked me to take a stress test, to insure my fitness for such a high profile assignment. I didn't object. The doctor who administered the exam told me the results were consistent with those of a healthy forty-year-old man. It appeared all systems were go, until my son Jim received a strange call from Jerry Becker at the NYSAC, who told him that, for reasons he could not discuss, I wasn't going to do the Hopkins–Trinidad fight after all. It was all quite mysterious, and apparently the decision was steeped in boxing politics.

When Jim relayed the bad news to me I felt hurt but decided it was not worth a pitched battle. Friends and supporters of mine felt differently, however, and mounted a campaign to undo what they saw as a double-cross. The upshot was that I was offered the assignment to referee the Ricardo Lopez–Zolani Petelo fight for the Junior Flyweight Championship of the World, billed as the co-feature of Hopkins–Trinidad. I accepted with pleasure.

When I arrived in the city that night, there was an eerie stillness as if the great metropolis, shaken to the core by the September 11 attack on the Twin Towers, was waiting for the other shoe to drop. You could smell fear on the streets.

It was more than understandable. What happened September 11 was worse than the attack on Pearl Harbor. I knew no one who died at Pearl Harbor, a military installation thousands of miles away, but scores of people in my own hometown, people I saw at the local grocery store, coaching on the athletic fields and at Sunday Mass, were lost in the rubble of what had been the mighty Twin Towers. But enshrouded as we were by sorrow, there was also a breath of patriotism in the air the likes of which I have not seen since World War II.

America is so big and so strong that solicitousness for her welfare is not an attitude we are much accustomed to. It was only when our country was hurt, in danger and vulnerable that I and millions of other Americans realized anew how much we love this cherished land.

In contrast to the eerie silence outside, the packed Garden was brimming with life and enthusiasm. There's nothing like a big fight crowd to showcase the fighting spirit of America. The city was alive and well, and I knew then that, no matter what, we would prevail in the end.

This old guy had to step pretty lively to keep up with those 108-pounders, but I managed without any problem. I stopped the bout at 1:32 of the eighth round, declaring Ricardo Lopez the winner. I took satisfaction in the knowledge that I refereed that fight no differently than I would have fifty years earlier. When announcer Jim Lampley came to interview me, it really dawned on me that it was my last round. It was a fitting farewell. But I had no regrets, just a heart full of gratitude for such a rich and absorbing career.

Life had been good to me. My family, my career, my health was more than I possibly could have hoped for. Gloria and the boys surprised me with an eightieth birthday party, and my oldest son, Glenn, handed me the keys to my new Mercedes. I deserved it, he said, for all the jams I got him out of. "Are you kidding me, Glenn?" I joked with him. "A fleet of Mercedes would hardly be compensation."

The hardest thing about getting older is the loss of so many cherished friends. A feeling of loneliness creeps upon you when you realize there are so few left to talk over old times with. I recently lost one of my dearest friends, the boxing writer Colonel Robert Thornton. Over the past thirty years, we spoke almost every day and would often lunch together. Bob seemed destined for boxing. When he was eighteen months old, Bob's father took him to a temperance meeting where former heavyweight champion John L. Sullivan, a reformed alcoholic, was speaking. The great John L. liked to mix with his audience and, as Bob's father often recounted, playfully shook baby Bob's hand. I would joke with Bob about the old boxing boast of shaking the hand that shook the hand of John L. Sullivan.

Bob had eleven bootleg fights, winning ten straight, before he was badly cut and hung up the gloves for the mightier pen. I never met anyone so hard to know and no one more worth making the effort for. He was the most honest, genuine, incorruptible human being I ever knew.

Sometimes Stan Weston, former boxing editor of *The Ring* magazine, would join us. Bob and Stan had been friends for sixty years and grew up in the business together. We had great times; both men were enormously talented and amazingly knowledgeable boxing historians.

The conversation never lagged, neither did the companionship. For my eightieth birthday they presented me with a photograph of the three of us with this inscription penned by Stan:

> *Bob and Stan, who have already been inducted into the royal order of the 80s, hereby and officially, welcome "The Third Member of the Saintly Musketeers" into the Sacred Order. Let's shoot for the 90s.*

It wasn't to be. Stan passed on six months before Bob.

In my retirement I have not completely exited the stage. I do my best to keep fit, age as gracefully as I can, think positive and go forward. And yes, I still go to fights sometimes as a boxing judge. When I was a referee I really enjoyed scoring a bout—back when we had that responsibility—and it's nice to be turning in a score card again. In truth, I *do* miss being inside the ropes, but the sport I love is still very much a part of my life. I talk with fans at boxing shows and attend fights as a spectator—particularly when Arthur Jr. is refereeing; critiquing my son is an old habit that's hard to break. In the end, I can think of no better way to go about the rest of my life than to live it in much the same way I refereed a fight, "in the scene, but unseen."

appendix
SELECTED MAJOR BOUTS
Refereed by Arthur Mercante

Sanctioning Bodies for Titles:

IBF = International Boxing Federation
NYSAC = New York State Athletic Commission
WBA = World Boxing Association
WBC = World Boxing Council
world = a consensus or unified world title

RESULTS KEY:

RES = results
RDS = rounds
dec = judges' decision
KO = knockout
TKO = technical knockout
D = draw

DATE–TITLE CONTESTED/SITE	WINNER/LOSER	RES/RDS
6/20/60–World Heavyweight Polo Grounds, New York	Floyd Patterson Ingemar Johansson	KO 5*
12/10/60–World Welterweight Madison Square Garden, New York	Benny 'Kid' Paret Luis Federico Thompson	dec 15
3/30/65–World Welterweight Madison Square Garden, New York	Emile Griffith Jose Stable	dec 15
12/10/65–World Welterweight Madison Square Garden, New York	Emile Griffith Manuel Gonzalez	dec 15
4/25/66–World Middleweight Madison Square Garden, New York	Emile Griffith Dick Tiger	dec 15
1/23/67–World Middleweight Madison Square Garden, New York	Emile Griffith Joey Archer	dec 15
8/16/67–World Lightweight Shea Stadium, Flushing, NY	Carlos Ortiz Ismael Laguna	dec 15
1/28/68–WBC Flyweight Mexico City	Chartchai Chionoi Efren Torres	TKO 13
3/4/68–NYSAC World Heavyweight Madison Square Garden, New York	Joe Frazier Buster Mathis	TKO 11
6/24/68–NYSAC World Heavyweight Madison Square Garden, New York	Joe Frazier Manuel Ramos	TKO 2
10/25/68–N/A Madison Square Garden, New York	Dick Tiger Frank DePaula	dec 10*

*Fight of the Year—*The Ring

DATE–TITLE CONTESTED/SITE	WINNER/LOSER	RES/RDS
2/23/69–WBC Flyweight El Toreo Bullring, Mexico City	**Efren Torres** Chartchai Chionoi	TKO 8
6/23/69–NYSAC World Heavyweight Madison Square Garden, New York	**Joe Frazier** Jerry Quarry	TKO 7*
3/20/70–WBC Flyweight Bangkok	**Chartchai Chionoi** Efren Torres	dec 15
2/12/71–World Lightweight Sports Arena, Los Angeles	**Ken Buchanan** Ruben Navarro	dec 15
3/8/71–World Heavyweight Madison Square Garden, New York	**Joe Frazier** Muhammad Ali	dec 15*
6/16/72–NYSAC World Welterweight War Memorial Aud., Syracuse, NY	**Hedgemon Lewis** Billy Backus	dec 15
1/22/73–World Heavyweight National Stadium, Kingston, Jamaica	**George Foreman** Joe Frazier	TKO 2*
9/28/76–World Heavyweight Yankee Stadium, Bronx, NY	**Muhammad Ali** Ken Norton	dec 15
8/3/77–NYSAC World Light Welterweight Madison Square Garden, New York	**Wilfred Benitez** Ray Guerrero	TKO 15
9/10/77–WBC Super Featherweight San Juan, Puerto Rico	**Alfredo Escalera** Sigfredo Rodriguez	dec 15
1/28/78–WBC Super Featherweight Loubriel Stadium, San Juan, PR	**Alexis Arguello** Alfredo Escalera	TKO 13
10/26/79–WBC Super Bantamweight Madison Square Garden, New York	**Wilfredo Gomez** Nicky Perez	TKO 5
3/31/80–WBC Welterweight Capital Centre, Landover, MD	**Sugar Ray Leonard** Davey "Boy" Green	KO 4
7/12/80–WBC Junior Middleweight Empire Pool, London	**Maurice Hope** Rocky Mattioli	TKO 11
11/1/80–WBC Lightweight Kelvin Hall, Glasgow, Scotland	**Jim Watt** Sean O'Grady	TKO 12
11/26/80–WBC Junior Middleweight Empire Pool, London	**Maurice Hope** Carlos Maria del Valle Herrera	dec 15
3/28/81–WBC Welterweight Carrier Dome, Syracuse, NY	**Sugar Ray Leonard** Larry Bonds	TKO 10

Date–Title Contested/Site	Winner/Loser	Res/Rds
6/20/81–WBC Lightweight Empire Pool, London	Alexis Arguello Jim Watt	dec 15
8/29/81–WBC Super Featherweight Stadio de Pini, Viareggio, Italy	Rolando Navarrete Cornelius Boza Edwards	KO 5
11/7/81–WBA Junior Middleweight Memorial Aud., Rochester, NY	Tadashi Mihara Rocky Fratto	dec 15
12/19/81–WBC Light Heavyweight Playboy Hotel, Atlantic City	Dwight Muhammad Qawi Matthew Saad Muhammad	TKO 10
12/3/82–WBC Super Bantamweight Superdome, New Orleans	Wilfredo Gomez Lupe Pintor	TKO 14
5/1/83–WBC Lightweight R. Clemente Coliseum, San Juan, PR	Edwin Rosario Jose Luis Ramirez	dec 12
6/25/83–WBC Featherweight R. Clemente Coliseum, San Juan, PR	Juan LaPorte Johnny De La Rosa	dec 12
2/4/84–WBA/IBF Welterweight Bally's Park Place, Atlantic City	Donald Curry Marlon Starling	dec 15
4/7/84–WBA Bantamweight Sands Hotel, Atlantic City	Richie Sandoval Jeff Chandler	TKO 15
9/15/84–WBC Junior Middleweight Civic Center, Saginaw, MI	Thomas Hearns Fred Hutchings	TKO 3
10/19/84–World Middleweight Madison Square Garden, New York	Marvin Hagler Mustafa Hamsho	TKO 3
2/16/85–WBC Super Lightweight Midtown Center, Kingston, NY	Billy Costello Leroy Haley	dec 12
4/27/85–WBC Junior Flyweight Hyundai Gymnasium, Ulsan, South Korea	Jung Koo Chang German Torres	dec 12
1/18/86–WBC Super Bantamweight Hua Mark Indoor Stadium, Bangkok	Samart Payakaroon Lupe Pintor	KO 5
6/13/86–WBC Lightweight Madison Square Garden, New York	Hector Camacho Edwin Rosario	dec 12
12/2/86–WBC Super Lightweight Kokugikan, Tokyo	Tsuyoshi Hamada Ronnie Shields	dec 12
5/8/87–WBC Super Bantamweight Entertainment Centre, Sydney	Jeff Fenech Samart Payakaroon	KO 4

Date–Title Contested/Site	Winner/Loser	Res/Rds
10/10/87–WBC Lightweight Zenith Théâtre, Paris	Jose Luis Ramirez Cornelius Boza Edwards	KO 5
3/21/88–World Heavyweight Tokyo Dome, Tokyo	Mike Tyson Tony Tubbs	TKO 2
11/30/88–WBC Featherweight National Tennis Centre, Melbourne	Jeff Fenech Georgie Navarro	TKO 5
7/8/89–WBC Junior Middleweight Mirapolis, Cergy-Pontoise, France	John Mugabi Rene Jacquot	TKO 1
9/15/89–WBC Welterweight Civic Center, Hartford, CT	Marlon Starling Yung Kil Chung	dec 12
11/7/89–WBC Super Flyweight Arena Mexico, Mexico City	Nana Konadu Gilberto Roman	dec 12
12/16/89–WBC Super Lightweight Palacio de los Deportes, Mexico City	Julio Cesar Chavez Alberto de las Mercedes Cortes	TKO 3
6/2/90–WBC Featherweight Leisure Centre, Manchester, England	Marcos Villasana Paul Hodkinson	TKO 8
7/28/90–WBC Light Heavyweight Rod Laver Arena, Melbourne	Dennis Andries Jeff Harding	KO 7
1/19/91–WBA Welterweight Convention Center, Atlantic City	Meldrick Taylor Aaron Davis	dec 12
7/20/91–WBC Cruiserweight Palermo, Italy	Anaclet Wamba Massimiliano Duran	TKO 11
3/1/92–WBC Super Featherweight Princes Park, Melbourne	Azumah Nelson Jeff Fenech	TKO 8
4/10/92–WBC Super Lightweight Plaza El Toreo, Mexico City	Julio Cesar Chavez Angel Hernandez	TKO 5
6/25/92–WBC Welterweight Acquaflash di Licola, Licola, Italy	James McGirt Patrizio Oliva	dec 12
12/3/92–WBC Light Heavyweight S. Franklin, St. Jean De Luz, France	Jeff Harding David Vedder	dec 12
4/28/93–WBC Featherweight National Boxing Stadium, Dublin	Gregorio Vargas Paul Hodkinson	TKO 7
9/19/93–WBC Minimumweight Capitol City Discotheque, Bangkok	Ricardo Lopez Toto Pongsawang	TKO 11

Date–Title Contested/Site	Winner/Loser	Res/Rds
12/18/93–WBC Super Lightweight Estadio Cuauhtemoc, Puebla, Mex.	Julio Cesar Chavez Andy Holligan	TKO 5
3/29/94–WBC Lightweight Palais Cerdan, Levallois-Perret, Fr.	Miguel Angel Gonzalez Jean Baptiste Mendy	TKO 5
5/6/94–WBC Heavyweight Convention Center, Atlantic City	Lennox Lewis Phil Jackson	TKO 8
1/18/95–WBC Super Flyweight Bunka Gym, Yokohama, Japan	Hiroshi Kawashima Jose Luis Bueno	dec 12
6/2/95–WBC Super Bantamweight Foxwoods, Mashantucket, CT	Hector Acero Sanchez Daniel Zaragoza	D 12
1/13/96–WBC Light Heavyweight Palais des Spec., St. Etienne, France	Fabrice Tiozzo Eric Lucas	dec 12
7/6/96–WBC Featherweight Luneta Park, Manila	Luisito Espinosa Cesar Soto	dec 12
10/4/96–WBA Welterweight Madison Square Garden, New York	Ike Quartey Oba Carr	dec 12
4/14/97–WBC Super Bantamweight Prefectural Gym, Osaka, Japan	Daniel Zaragoza Joichiro Tatsuyoshi	dec 12
8/7/97–WBC Light Heavyweight Foxwoods, Mashantucket, CT	Roy Jones Jr Montell Griffin	TKO 1
3/7/98–WBC/WBA Minimumweight Plaza de Toros, Mexico City	Rosendo Alvarez Ricardo Lopez	D 8
11/14/98–WBC/WBA Light Heavyweight Foxwoods, Mashantucket, CT	Roy Jones Jr Otis Grant	TKO 10
9/24/99–WBC Middleweight MCI Center, Washington, DC	Keith Holmes Andrew Council	dec 12
1/15/00–World Light Heavyweight Radio City Music Hall, New York	Roy Jones Jr David Telesco	dec 12
11/4/00–WBC Welterweight MSG Theatre, New York	Shane Mosley Antonio Diaz	TKO 6
1/13/01–IBF Junior Welterweight Mohegan Sun, Uncasville, CT	Zab Judah Reggie Green	TKO 10
9/29/01–IBF Junior Flyweight Madison Square Garden, New York	Ricardo Lopez Zolani Petelo	KO 8

INDEX